Reader's Digest · National Trust

Nature Notebooks

WOODLAND TREES AND SHRUBS

Reader's Digest · National Trust

Nature Notebooks

WOODLAND TREES AND SHRUBS

Published by The Reader's Digest Association Limited, London,
in association with The National Trust

WOODLAND TREES AND SHRUBS
is a Reader's Digest Publication based upon The Reader's Digest
Nature Lover's Library Copyright © 1981 The Reader's Digest
Association Limited, London

First Edition
Copyright © 1986
The Reader's Digest Association Limited
25 Berkeley Square
London W1X 6AB

Additional editorial work by Duncan Petersen Publishing Limited,
5 Botts Mews, London W2 5AG.
Typesetting by Modern Reprographics Ltd, Hull, North Humberside.
Separations by Modern Reprographics Ltd, (covers) and Mullis
Morgan Ltd, London (duplicate film)
Printed by Everbest Printing Company Limited in Hong Kong

The illustration on the cover is of Selborne Hill by Michael Woods.

CONTENTS

Using this book

The British Isles are host to a wonderful variety of woodlands and plantations and it is everyone's good fortune that of these all the most interesting types may be seen on properties owned and managed by The National Trust.

This book takes advantage of that happy coincidence by being not only a field guide to woodland trees and shrubs, but also a gazetteer of National Trust sites where there is every opportunity to see the species, indeed not just to see them, but to observe some of the finest specimens of their kind. Because the National Trust manages its property (see opposite) and because public access is almost always easy, making a special journey to any of the sites described is a worthwhile end in itself.

The page references

In a box on each colour plate page in the field guide section you will find a brief general note on each species and then a sequence of numbers, and it is these which are the key to the book's dual function as identification guide and sites gazetteer. The numbers simply direct you to sites where you will see the species in question. They are not the only sites listed where you can see that species; but they are ones which the book's editor has singled out as being especially worth a visit for that species in particular; often the sites boast especially large, or beautiful examples of the tree or shrub in question; often, too, they will be among the select few places in the British Isles where a rare species can be seen. Equally, you will find some species cross-referenced to a site, but not

mentioned in the site description: this is because space in the gazetteer allows mention only of key species.

Choice of species

Illustrated in the field guide section on pages 12-95 are trees and shrubs most of which grow somewhere on a wooded property owned by the National Trust, the National Trust for Scotland, or in one of the Republic of Ireland's national woodlands. The book features not only those tall trees which with their leafy tops comprise the 'roof' or canopy of woodland, but also those generally shorter species which make up the shrub layer on the woodland floor.

The majority of trees and shrubs illustrated are common and familiar in British woodlands and plantations, but among them there are a few surprises: typically, species which have seeded themselves in woodland from nearby gardens, and these 'rogue' or 'imposter' species provide an interesting extra dimension to the coverage.

Many fine ornamental trees grow alongside woodland trees on National Trust properties, and you will find references to them in the sites gazetteer when it seems particularly appropriate. If you are interested in ornamental trees the perfect companion to this book is its sister volume in the Reader's Digest National Trust *Nature Notebook* series – *Ornamental Trees*. It is organized in exactly the same way as this book, with familiar ornamental tree species featured in full colour for easy identification, plus references to National Trust sites described in the same helpful detail at the back of the book.

The nomenclature used for the species corresponds to that in the Reader's Digest *Field Guide to the Trees and Shrubs of Britain.*

The 'notebook' panels

Making records of field observations is an excellent habit: it makes identification easier the next time round if you stop to think about, and record, the features which enabled you to name a species; and it will bring back happy memories of days out. The space left blank for your notes at the foot of each page is intended as an introduction to making field notes; many will want to develop it further by buying a full-size notebook. Perhaps the most important section of the notebook panel is that left blank for sketches: however amateur you may think your efforts in this direction, they *are* worth making, for a drawing, however feeble, forces you to observe in detail.

Help for visitors

Many of the National Trust's woodland trees and shrubs grow in parks and gardens where expert staff are on hand to answer queries and guide visitors to the specimens they want to see. An added bonus may also be the presence of well-signposted nature walks, designed to take you round the key features of the property; and of course, there are also likely to be such amenities as car parks, information centres, shops, tea rooms and even play areas for children.

Of course, the Trust owns numerous isolated, completely tranquil woodlands, many of which are featured in the sites gazetteer. They have the excellent advantage of being accessible at most, if not all, times, and a visit can usually be made to such sites without worrying about opening times.

Choice of sites

Every site featured in the gazetteer section has been chosen in conjunction with a top horticultural expert to give an interesting and representative cross-section of Trust properties. A significant portion are sites which are readily accessible from major centres of population, or which are in parts of the country favoured by visiting holidaymakers.

Opening hours and admission

The times of opening, and the admission fees are those which were current at time of going to press. The National Trust and The National Trust for Scotland review their admission fees each year, so that in general there is the possibility of a modest increase over the sum stated in this book.

Full information on opening hours and admission fees is published in the following annual publications: *National Trust Properties Open,* the National Trust for Scotland's *Guide to over 100 Properties,* and the Historic Irish Tourist Houses and Gardens Association's *Historic Houses, Castles and Gardens Open to the Public.*

Many National Trust properties comprise an historic house and grounds; prices given generally refer to admission to both house and grounds, but in some cases special arrangements are available for those who wish to enter the grounds only for natural history purposes.

THE NATIONAL TRUST –
WOODLAND MANAGEMENT,
PRESENT AND FUTURE

The National Trust and the National Trust for Scotland (a separate organization, but with similar aims) own many thousands of acres of woodlands throughout Great Britain and Northern Ireland. Their first concern is to preserve the landscape and open their properties for their members and the general public to enjoy. They are also well aware of the wildlife value of their woods, and nature conservation is another important objective of their woodland management. Timber production, regarded by many as the traditional purpose of forestry, is of lesser priority in their case, but it is practised wherever it does not conflict with their other objectives, to provide a range of useful products from fence posts to large constructional timbers and a valuable source of income.

The Trusts' woodland management is designed to balance these varied and sometimes conflicting objectives. The greatest need is to introduce young trees into old and often neglected woods, in order gradually to regenerate them with the least disturbance to their landscape and wildlife value. Trees must be felled as they mature, both to produce timber and to provide space for their successors to grow. But as far as possible, felling areas are kept small and irregular, and the new plantings are usually composed of similar trees to those they replace; conifer woods are normally regenerated with conifers and broad-leaves with broad-leaves, though in some cases conifers may be mixed with the slower-growing young broad-leaves to act as a 'nurse' in their early years. Small-scale working, the avoidance of large areas of clear felling, and the introduction of diversity both of species and age classes all help to ensure that woods are maintained and perpetuated with the minimum of disturbance to their appearance in the landscape or to the fragile plant and animal habitats which they contain.

This book will help you to explore our woods and recognize the rich variety of trees and shrubs which can be found in them. Some are native, many more have been introduced from all over the world; all are part of our heritage which the National Trusts are helping to protect for us and for the future.

Dr T.W. Wright, *Adviser on Conservation and Woodlands, The National Trust.*

Basic fieldcraft

KEY TO BROAD-LEAVED TREES

The trees and shrubs illustrated and described in the main part of this book have been grouped according to the shape of their leaves; for throughout most of the year this provides the single most obvious clue by which to identify them. When trying to put a name to a tree or shrub, first compare its leaves with those illustrated in this key.

Oval leaves

Heart-shaped leaves

Triangular leaves

Long leaves

Round leaves

If there is a failsafe piece of advice for the would-be naturalist, it is never to try to learn too much at once. This holds particularly true for those who want to identify, and observe trees for, unlike birds and insects, they have the advantage of not rushing about. There is all the time in the world to study them.

Absolutely basic to successful tree identification is a notebook, or a space for notes, such as provided in this book, and a sharp pencil. If you have a camera, take that along too. Notes are essential because, although you may think you can remember all the necessary details, it is amazing how quickly they become blurred. If you can make a few sketches, they should help, as will photographs.

Once confronted by your chosen tree what you look for to assist identification will largely be determined by the time of year; which is why the panel left blank in the *Nature Notebook* has a space specifically for the date. However, a useful first step, no matter what the season, is to take an overall look. Note the height and general shape (remembering that if a tree is closely surrounded by others this will affect its growth and shape).

Next consider whether your tree is broad-leaved or coniferous. Most broad-leaved trees shed their leaves in winter –

Maple-like leaves

Hand-shaped leaves

Feather-like leaves

Lobed leaves

Unusual leaves
(Not featured in this book; see the companion *Nature Notebook, Ornamental Trees.*)

in other words, they are deciduous. The leaves of conifers are either needle-like or small and scale-like, and mostly evergreen. Notable exceptions to this rule are holly and larch. The fact that most coniferous trees are evergreen means that you are looking for more or less the same basic clues to identification all the year round: if it has needles, are they long or short and are they grouped in twos, threes or more? Are they hard or soft, dark or pale green? If a conifer has small, hard leaves, note their arrangement, texture and colour. Are they in opposite pairs or alternate? Are they, for example, bright green, yellowish or dark green? Crush some of the foliage and try to remember the smell. It can be most distinctive. Are there any flowers on the tree, and if so, what are they like? The general appearance of the cones can also help. Again, all these factors will, with the help of the field guide pages in this book, narrow down the range of possible identifications.

If your tree is broad-leaved, make a special point of examining the twigs and leaf buds in winter and early spring. See whether the twigs are straight or angled, rough or smooth. Are the leaf buds opposite each other, alternate or even in a spiral? Note their shape, colour and general formation. In spring and sum-

KEY TO CONIFEROUS TREES

The leaves of coniferous trees can be divided into those which are needle-like and those which resemble scales. Trees with scale-like leaves sometimes also have awl-shaped juvenile leaves which persist on the adult tree. The needle-like leaves fall into four groups. Pines have long needles in groups of two, three or five. Spruce needles are sharp and arise on pegs. The needles of cedars and larches are in rosettes on the older twigs; those of larches are deciduous. Other trees have flat needles, including the silver firs whose needles leave a round leaf scar.

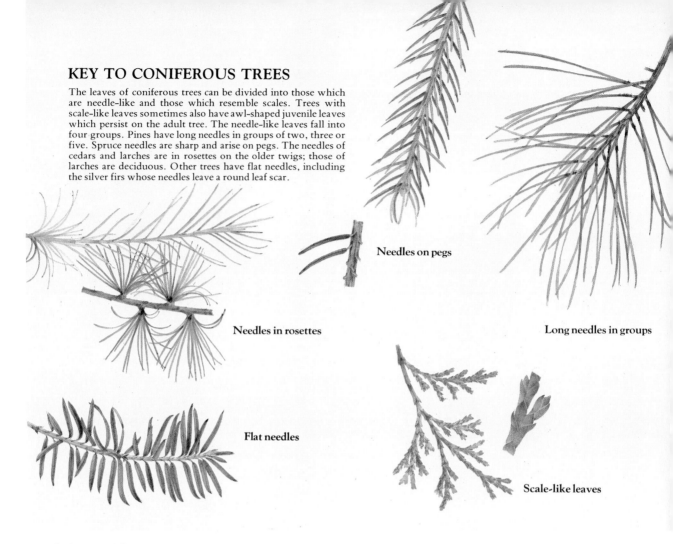

Needles on pegs

Needles in rosettes

Long needles in groups

Flat needles

Scale-like leaves

mer, the leaves and flowers are obviously the most important guides. Is the tree flowering before it has come into leaf? Are the flowers insignificant or showy? Are there two types of flowers (male and female) on the same tree or are they on separate trees? Look closely because the female flowers are often small and difficult to spot.

The leaves of deciduous trees can comprise a single blade (simple) or they can be made up of several parts (compound). How are they arranged on the twigs? What shape are they? Are the edges smooth, serrated or jagged? What size are they and what colour? When it comes to colour remember that fresh, new leaves are often quite different to the mature leaves and will probably change yet again in the autumn.

Autumn, of course, brings the main avalanche or nuts, seeds, berries and acorns, an enormous aid to positive identification. Determine whether the fruits are single or in bunches, soft, or in shells. Are the shells hard, prickly or smooth? Do the fruits sit in cups, as the acorns do, and, if so, are the cups smooth or hairy and do they sit directly on the twigs or do they have long stalks?

Once you start observing closely, you will notice much more than just these basic points.

THE TREES AND SHRUBS

An identification guide to 84 species

●

The species are grouped according to the shape of their leaves or needles – see the explanatory key opposite, and on pages 8-9.

●

If you already know the name of a species and want to look it it up, simply consult the index.

●

In this *Nature Notebook* a few of the trees and all of the shrubs are given no site references. This is usually because they are generally distributed, likely to be seen on most of the sites in the gazetteer section. In some cases, however, it is because the species are uncommon in woodland, and have been included as points of exceptional or general interest.

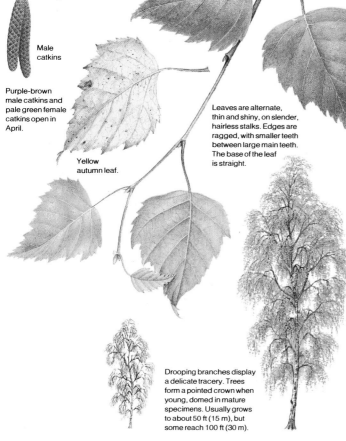

Female catkins

Male catkins

Purple-brown male catkins and pale green female catkins open in April.

Yellow autumn leaf.

Leaves are alternate, thin and shiny, on slender, hairless stalks. Edges are ragged, with smaller teeth between large main teeth. The base of the leaf is straight.

Drooping branches display a delicate tracery. Trees form a pointed crown when young, domed in mature specimens. Usually grows to about 50 ft (15 m), but some reach 100 ft (30 m).

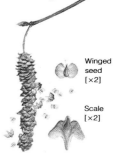

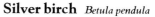

Winged seed [×2]

Scale [×2]

Fruiting catkins stay on the tree until winter, when they break up into scales and winged, wind-borne seeds.

Silver birch *Betula pendula*

Its straight silvery-white trunk and pendulous branches make the silver birch one of the most decorative and easily recognised of Britain's native trees. Despite its delicate appearance it is one of the world's hardiest trees, and in Britain, with rowan, will grow higher up mountains than any other deciduous tree. It grows particularly well on the sands and gravels of south-eastern England, and is often planted as an ornamental tree in gardens and streets, where its small size is an advantage.

The silver birch was a holy tree, revered by pagan Celtic and Germanic tribes: in Britain the Druids gave its name to a midwinter month. The birch was considered to have sacred powers of renewal and purification, so its twigs were used in the ritual of driving out the spirits of the old year. The belief persisted into historical times, when delinquents and the insane were birched to expel evil spirits.

The timber of silver birch shows no distinction between heartwood and sapwood. It is made into the backs of brushes and tool handles; it does not grow big enough in Britain for commercial use as timber. Birch twigs are cut in winter to make besom brooms for gardens and forest-fire beaters.

Location

Date

Habitat

Sketches

Winter reveals fewer and thicker branches than on silver birch. 80 ft (24 m).

Catkins open in April; females smaller and more erect than males.

Female catkin

Male catkin

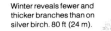
Veins on underside of leaf are hairy; teeth are more even in size than on silver birch leaves. Base is triangular, the stalk slender and hairy.

The branches of this round-headed tree are twisting, and seldom hang down.

Seed [Actual size]

Yellow autumn leaf.

Scale [Actual size]

Fruit stays on tree in winter, breaking up into scales and winged seeds. The seeds are wind-borne.

Downy birch *Betula pubescens*

One of two birches native to the British Isles, the downy birch frequently crosses with the silver birch, the other native species, to produce hybrids that have the characteristics of both. All are closely related to a Canadian birch, the bark of which was used by the Indians to cover their canoes and dwellings. The bark of these birches is waterproof and resistant to fungus; often it can be seen as a shell, left intact round the collapsed and rotting wood of the tree.

In upland areas, downy birch woods provide useful shelter for sheep in winter, and they are a favourite habitat for roe deer. Birches are short-lived, but play an important role as colonisers of poor soils. The wind-blown seed is easily spread and quickly forms scrub woodland, while the fallen leaves improve the soil for trees that need more favourable conditions.

The sap of the birch is rich in sugar. Tapped in spring it can be made into birch wine by adding honey, or it may be used as shampoo. Birch oil is obtained from the bark and used as insect repellent. The wood is soft, and though it rots quickly out of doors, it can be used for furniture, tool handles and plywood. As firewood it burns with a particularly bright flame.

Location	Sketches
Date	
Habitat	

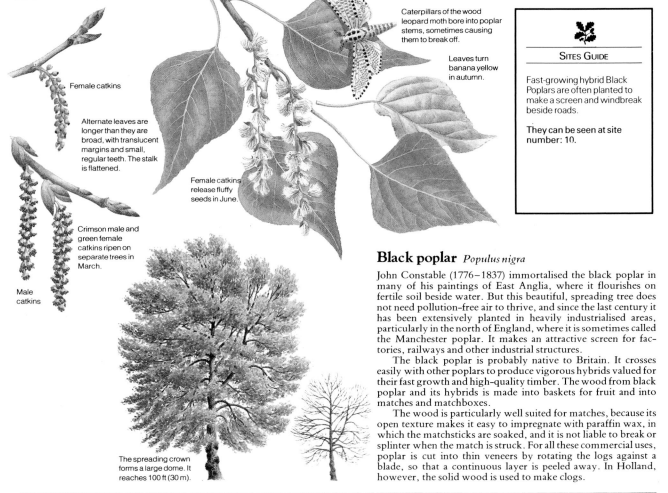

Caterpillars of the wood leopard moth bore into poplar stems, sometimes causing them to break off.

Female catkins

Alternate leaves are longer than they are broad, with translucent margins and small, regular teeth. The stalk is flattened.

Female catkins release fluffy seeds in June.

Leaves turn banana yellow in autumn.

Crimson male and green female catkins ripen on separate trees in March.

Male catkins

The spreading crown forms a large dome. It reaches 100 ft (30 m).

SITES GUIDE

Fast-growing hybrid Black Poplars are often planted to make a screen and windbreak beside roads.

They can be seen at site number: 10.

Black poplar *Populus nigra*

John Constable (1776–1837) immortalised the black poplar in many of his paintings of East Anglia, where it flourishes on fertile soil beside water. But this beautiful, spreading tree does not need pollution-free air to thrive, and since the last century it has been extensively planted in heavily industrialised areas, particularly in the north of England, where it is sometimes called the Manchester poplar. It makes an attractive screen for factories, railways and other industrial structures.

The black poplar is probably native to Britain. It crosses easily with other poplars to produce vigorous hybrids valued for their fast growth and high-quality timber. The wood from black poplar and its hybrids is made into baskets for fruit and into matches and matchboxes.

The wood is particularly well suited for matches, because its open texture makes it easy to impregnate with paraffin wax, in which the matchsticks are soaked, and it is not liable to break or splinter when the match is struck. For all these commercial uses, poplar is cut into thin veneers by rotating the logs against a blade, so that a continuous layer is peeled away. In Holland, however, the solid wood is used to make clogs.

Location

Date

Habitat

Sketches

Large, thick leaves have a white, metallic-looking underside and small regular teeth. There is no translucent margin. The leaves, like the sticky buds, have a strong sweet smell.

Leaf in autumn.

Flowers appear as catkins in March. Female catkins are long and green; male catkins, on separate trees, are shorter and dull crimson.

Male catkin

Female catkin

Woolly female catkins break up into fluffy seeds in May.

Regularly spaced branches give the tree a cone shape. It reaches 110 ft (33 m).

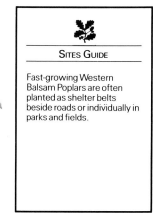

Western balsam poplar *Populus trichocarpa*

A growth rate of up to 6 ft a year makes the western balsam poplar one of the fastest-growing trees planted in Britain. It is a native of the western seaboard of North America, and is planted in Britain as an ornamental tree or to form a screen. Its soft wood, light in weight and colour, is used like other poplars for making matches, packing cases and baskets.

In spring, the tree's buds and young leaves exude a sticky substance, or balsam, with a heady, sweet odour that pervades the surrounding air. On hot, still days the smell carries for 100 yds or more.

Like all poplars, the western balsam requires low-lying, moist soil, and it can tolerate acid ground better than related European species. However, as a strong, fast grower, it needs freedom from competition from other trees, so it must be planted with plenty of space. Its roots die if the soil is stagnant and waterlogged. The main stem and branches are susceptible to ugly cankers, or growths, which detract from its decorative appeal, but it has been successfully crossed with other species to produce canker-resistant hybrids suitable for planting in parks or in corners of fields.

Location

Date

Habitat

Sketches

15

Male
catkins

Male and female catkins
grow on separate trees
and ripen in March.

Female
catkin

The grey poplar is
distinguished by
its open crown,
and by the white
of the upper bark
and the undersides
of the leaves. It
grows to about
75 ft (23 m).

Leaves are alternate and
thick, and very variable in
shape. Felted hairs on the
underside of the leaf show
white when disturbed by
wind. The leaf stalk is
slightly flattened.

Tree in winter.

Sites Guide

The Grey Poplar flourishes on
ground that is constantly
damp, particularly in water-
meadows and river valleys.

**It can be seen at site
number: 28.**

Grey poplar *Populus canescens*

Experts cannot agree whether the grey poplar is a species in its
own right or an ancient hybrid between the native aspen and the
introduced white poplar. Certainly it has features in common
with both species, but there are also noticeable differences. The
leaf of the grey poplar is much rounder than that of the white
poplar, and the down on the underside of the leaves, from which
it gets its name, is grey rather than white. The leaves of the
aspen, by contrast, are smooth on both sides.

The grey poplar is more tolerant of shade than other poplars
and occurs in damp woods, where the young suckers it sends up
from its roots often form dense thickets. It grows taller than the
white poplar, producing a straight white upper trunk which, in
maturity, is branchless for most of its height and pitted with
lines of black diamonds. Like white poplar, the tree is resistant to
salt-laden winds and is therefore often used to form shelter belts
near the sea.

When dry, the wood of grey poplar is tough, and nails can be
driven in without splitting it. It is used for packing cases and
storage pallets. The sapwood is very white, contrasting with the
dark brown heartwood.

Location	Sketches
Date	
Habitat	

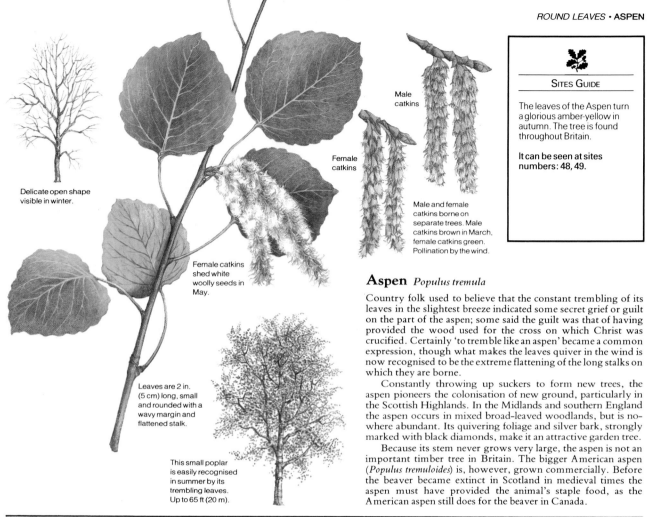

Delicate open shape
visible in winter.

Male
catkins

Female
catkins

Female catkins
shed white
woolly seeds in
May.

Leaves are 2 in.
(5 cm) long, small
and rounded with a
wavy margin and
flattened stalk.

This small poplar
is easily recognised
in summer by its
trembling leaves.
Up to 65 ft (20 m).

Male and female
catkins borne on
separate trees. Male
catkins brown in March,
female catkins green.
Pollination by the wind.

Aspen *Populus tremula*

Country folk used to believe that the constant trembling of its
leaves in the slightest breeze indicated some secret grief or guilt
on the part of the aspen; some said the guilt was that of having
provided the wood used for the cross on which Christ was
crucified. Certainly 'to tremble like an aspen' became a common
expression, though what makes the leaves quiver in the wind is
now recognised to be the extreme flattening of the long stalks on
which they are borne.

Constantly throwing up suckers to form new trees, the
aspen pioneers the colonisation of new ground, particularly in
the Scottish Highlands. In the Midlands and southern England
the aspen occurs in mixed broad-leaved woodlands, but is nowhere abundant. Its quivering foliage and silver bark, strongly
marked with black diamonds, make it an attractive garden tree.

Because its stem never grows very large, the aspen is not an
important timber tree in Britain. The bigger American aspen
(*Populus tremuloides*) is, however, grown commercially. Before
the beaver became extinct in Scotland in medieval times the
aspen must have provided the animal's staple food, as the
American aspen still does for the beaver in Canada.

Location	Sketches
Date	
Habitat	

Leaves are alternate, and up to 6 in. (15 cm) long. They are dark green and hairy on top, paler and densely hairy on the underside. The stalk is also hairy.

The flowers are sweet smelling. [× 2]

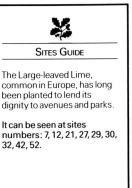

Three globe-shaped fruits usually hang on each bract. They are five-ribbed and covered with short hairs.

Greenish-yellow flowers, appearing in late June, before other limes, are a valuable source of nectar for bees. Flowers hang in clusters of three or four from long bracts.

This tall lime rises to 100 ft (30 m), with ascending branches and a narrow crown.

Large-leaved lime *Tilia platyphyllos*

Bees, moths, cattle and deer all make a feast of the lime tree, and the large-leaved lime, which flowers some weeks before other limes, draws bees to its nectar earlier than the rest. Lime seedlings are seldom seen in the wild, because they are very palatable to browsing animals. In parkland open to cattle or deer, older limes are often stripped of leaves to the height that the animals can reach. Lime leaves are popular, too, with the caterpillars of many moths, including the lime hawk moth, which lays its eggs on them early in May.

Nurserymen sometimes find it difficult to raise limes from seed, for unless it is gathered and sown as it ripens, it goes into dormancy and will not germinate easily. The seed of the large-leaved lime needs richer and damper soil than other limes if it is to flourish.

Once established, however, the lime is a hardy tree that graces many parks and public gardens. The large-leaved lime is long-lived and, unlike other limes, does not sprout at the base. Because it will stand hard pruning, it is a popular tree for planting in streets, especially in its red-twigged 'Rubra' form, which is more compact and erect.

Location

Date

Habitat

Sketches

Greenish-yellow flowers, sweet-smelling and attractive to bees, appear early in July in erect or spreading clusters of seven or eight on each bract.

Fruits are neither ribbed nor hairy like those of other limes.

Leaves are alternate and 1½–3 in. (4–7.5 cm) long. They are dark green and shiny on top, with orange tufts of hair in vein junctions on the undersides. The stalk is not hairy.

Downward-arching branches and a domed crown characterise this lime, which grows to 70 ft (22 m) high.

SITES GUIDE

The handsome Small-leaved Lime grows wild in Europe, and is a native tree of limestone soils in England and Wales.

It can be seen at sites numbers: 1, 22, 26, 29, 30, 32, 35-37.

Small-leaved lime *Tilia cordata*

Its decorative appearance has long made the small-leaved lime popular for planting in avenues; some of the trees that stand today in the grounds of Hampton Court Palace were planted by Charles I three and a half centuries ago. For humbler folk, the lime was a holy tree, ranged along village streets to protect the peasants against evil. Limes have been planted to give shade throughout man's history: records show that the ancient Greeks and Romans used the tree for this purpose.

Lime wood, being soft and even-grained, is ideal for carving and turning and has inspired generations of artists and craftsmen. The best known wood carver to use lime was Grinling Gibbons (1648–1721), whose work can still be seen in many of Britain's churches, cathedrals and great houses. The intricate and detailed portrayal of flowers and foliage for which Gibbons was celebrated would only have been possible with a fine-textured and easily worked wood such as lime.

Because it does not warp, lime wood is still used for the sounding boards and keys of pianos and organs. For the same reason it is a popular material for drawing boards. Fibres used to tie up plants are sometimes made from lime bark.

Location

Date

Habitat

Sketches

Leaves and clusters of yellow flowers grow on the short side-shoots, in the axils of the spines. The spines are grouped in threes. Leaves fall in winter.

SITES GUIDE

One of the most popular garden shrubs, Barberry is sometimes found in the wild in woods and hedges.

Hooker's barberry (*Berberis hookeri*) is an evergreen garden shrub with longer leaves; berries black.

The evergreen Darwin's barberry (*Berberis darwinii*) has holly-like leaves, small spines; berries blue.

In autumn the lozenge-shaped scarlet berries hang in bunches from the spiny twigs.

The purple-leaved cultivar 'Atropurpurea' is often grown in gardens for the sake of its colourful foliage.

Its thorny branches make the barberry a useful hedge. It grows to 10 ft (3 m) tall.

Barberry *Berberis vulgaris*

The sharp-thorned barberry has become rarer in the countryside in recent years, but it has won a new place as a decorative garden shrub. At one time barberry grew wild in hedgerows, and on commons and scrubland that was being re-invaded by wood-land. The shrub was, however, discovered to be a host to rust, a fungus that attacks the leaves and stems of wheat and other cereals, and it has been uprooted from grain-growing areas.

In country districts the barberry was prized for a variety of household uses. Its showy red berries, edible but tart and avoided by birds, are rich in vitamin C and can be made into jelly, jam or sweets. Barberry jams and jellies were given to sufferers from liver and stomach disorders. The leaves, too, are edible and can be added to salads or as seasoning to meats. In the Middle Ages, the bark was a source of yellow dye. The small size of the stems and branches limits the use of the hard yellow wood to inlay work.

Some 170 species and varieties of barberry, including the common wild barberry and the related purple-leaved barberry, flourish in Britain's gardens, either as ornamental plants or as hedges. They are easy to grow in most soils and situations.

Location

Date

Habitat

Sketches

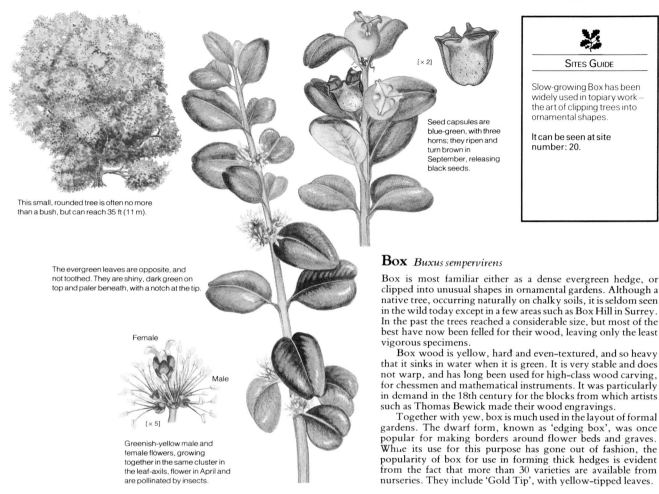

This small, rounded tree is often no more than a bush, but can reach 35 ft (11 m).

The evergreen leaves are opposite, and not toothed. They are shiny, dark green on top and paler beneath, with a notch at the tip.

Female

Male

[× 5]

Greenish-yellow male and female flowers, growing together in the same cluster in the leaf-axils, flower in April and are pollinated by insects.

[× 2]

Seed capsules are blue-green, with three horns; they ripen and turn brown in September, releasing black seeds.

SITES GUIDE

Slow-growing Box has been widely used in topiary work – the art of clipping trees into ornamental shapes.

It can be seen at site number: 20.

Box *Buxus sempervirens*

Box is most familiar either as a dense evergreen hedge, or clipped into unusual shapes in ornamental gardens. Although a native tree, occurring naturally on chalky soils, it is seldom seen in the wild today except in a few areas such as Box Hill in Surrey. In the past the trees reached a considerable size, but most of the best have now been felled for their wood, leaving only the least vigorous specimens.

Box wood is yellow, hard and even-textured, and so heavy that it sinks in water when it is green. It is very stable and does not warp, and has long been used for high-class wood carving, for chessmen and mathematical instruments. It was particularly in demand in the 18th century for the blocks from which artists such as Thomas Bewick made their wood engravings.

Together with yew, box is much used in the layout of formal gardens. The dwarf form, known as 'edging box', was once popular for making borders around flower beds and graves. While its use for this purpose has gone out of fashion, the popularity of box for use in forming thick hedges is evident from the fact that more than 30 varieties are available from nurseries. They include 'Gold Tip', with yellow-tipped leaves.

Location

Date

Habitat

Sketches

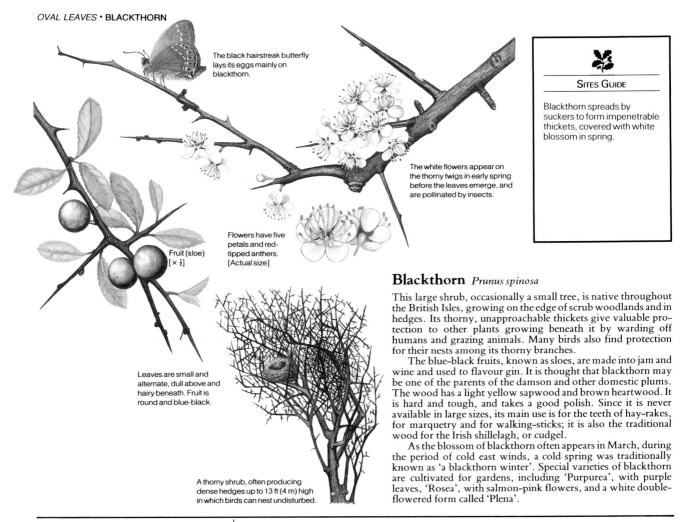

The black hairstreak butterfly lays its eggs mainly on blackthorn.

The white flowers appear on the thorny twigs in early spring before the leaves emerge, and are pollinated by insects.

Flowers have five petals and red-tipped anthers. [Actual size]

Fruit (sloe) [× ½]

Leaves are small and alternate, dull above and hairy beneath. Fruit is round and blue-black.

A thorny shrub, often producing dense hedges up to 13 ft (4 m) high in which birds can nest undisturbed.

SITES GUIDE

Blackthorn spreads by suckers to form impenetrable thickets, covered with white blossom in spring.

Blackthorn *Prunus spinosa*

This large shrub, occasionally a small tree, is native throughout the British Isles, growing on the edge of scrub woodlands and in hedges. Its thorny, unapproachable thickets give valuable protection to other plants growing beneath it by warding off humans and grazing animals. Many birds also find protection for their nests among its thorny branches.

The blue-black fruits, known as sloes, are made into jam and wine and used to flavour gin. It is thought that blackthorn may be one of the parents of the damson and other domestic plums. The wood has a light yellow sapwood and brown heartwood. It is hard and tough, and takes a good polish. Since it is never available in large sizes, its main use is for the teeth of hay-rakes, for marquetry and for walking-sticks; it is also the traditional wood for the Irish shillelagh, or cudgel.

As the blossom of blackthorn often appears in March, during the period of cold east winds, a cold spring was traditionally known as 'a blackthorn winter'. Special varieties of blackthorn are cultivated for gardens, including 'Purpurea', with purple leaves, 'Rosea', with salmon-pink flowers, and a white double-flowered form called 'Plena'.

Location	Sketches
Date	
Habitat	

Caterpillars of the holly blue butterfly feed on the leaves.

Leaves are alternate and evergreen, with sharp spines. They are glossy and waxy on top, matt and paler green beneath. Only female trees bear berries.

Male flower

The small, scented male and female flowers appear in May on separate trees. [Actual sizes]

Female flower

This narrow-crowned, conical tree has regular branching when young but becomes straggly with age. It can reach 65 ft (20 m).

'Bacciflava'

'Aureomarginata'

'Ferox'

There are many cultivated varieties with different shapes and leaf colours and variously coloured berries. Some are used for hedging, and others as ornamental trees.

'Lawsonia'

Holly *Ilex aquifolium*

Many a holly tree was spared the woodman's axe in days gone by because of a superstition that it was unlucky to cut down a holly tree. As a result, many hollies are today seen growing in the midst of hedgerows that have grown up around them. The superstition probably arose because of the tree's evergreen leaves and its long-lasting berries, leading people to associate the tree with eternity and the power to ward off evil and destruction. In addition, the holly has long been a symbol of Christmas.

Another tradition associated with the holly tree is that a good crop of berries is a warning of a hard winter on the way. This tradition probably arose out of the fondness shown by birds – especially thrushes – for the fruit as a source of food. In fact, a bumper crop of berries is not an augury of bad weather to come, but the result of a fine summer just past.

Holly is native to the British Isles, where it grows everywhere except on wet soils, tolerating conditions that would be too harsh for other trees. It forms a good hedge, and can be clipped and shaped. The wood of holly is white, sometimes with a greenish streak, and is dense, hard and heavy; like box it has been used for carving, inlay work and woodcuts.

Location

Date

Habitat

Sketches

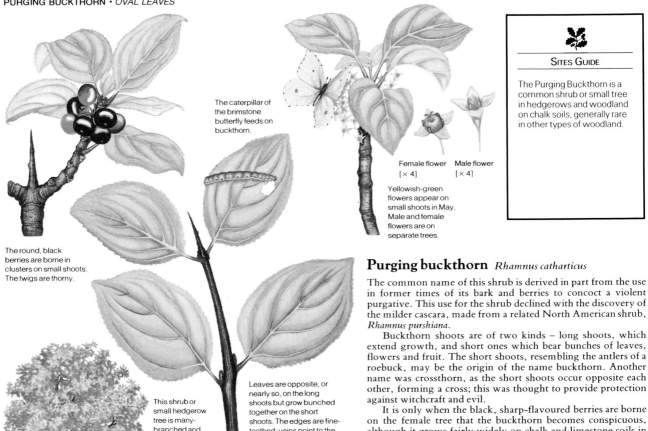

The round, black berries are borne in clusters on small shoots. The twigs are thorny.

The caterpillar of the brimstone butterfly feeds on buckthorn.

This shrub or small hedgerow tree is many-branched and thorny. Thick foliage grows close to the ground. The bark is rough and scaly. Up to 16 ft (5 m).

Leaves are opposite, or nearly so, on the long shoots but grow bunched together on the short shoots. The edges are fine-toothed; veins point to the tip of the leaf.

Female flower [× 4]   Male flower [× 4]

Yellowish-green flowers appear on small shoots in May. Male and female flowers are on separate trees.

Sites Guide

The Purging Buckthorn is a common shrub or small tree in hedgerows and woodland on chalk soils, generally rare in other types of woodland.

Purging buckthorn *Rhamnus catharticus*

The common name of this shrub is derived in part from the use in former times of its bark and berries to concoct a violent purgative. This use for the shrub declined with the discovery of the milder cascara, made from a related North American shrub, *Rhamnus purshiana*.

Buckthorn shoots are of two kinds – long shoots, which extend growth, and short ones which bear bunches of leaves, flowers and fruit. The short shoots, resembling the antlers of a roebuck, may be the origin of the name buckthorn. Another name was crossthorn, as the short shoots occur opposite each other, forming a cross; this was thought to provide protection against witchcraft and evil.

It is only when the black, sharp-flavoured berries are borne on the female tree that the buckthorn becomes conspicuous, although it grows fairly widely on chalk and limestone soils in central and southern England. It can stand a certain amount of shade. The sapwood is yellow and the heartwood reddish-brown. Nowadays the wood has no uses, but in Iron Age Britain it was cut and used with other woods such as oak for making the charcoal then necessary for smelting.

Location	Sketches
Date	
Habitat	

Alder Buckthorn grows in damp woods, in peaty soils and on raised bogs, where it often grows with alder. It is generally rare in woodland.

The berries turn from green to red and purple. Turning yellow in autumn, the leaves hang downwards before falling.

Alder buckthorn *Frangula alnus*

From explosives to laxatives, from dyestuffs to butchery, this attractive, shrubby little tree has served man in a variety of roles. Charcoal from its wood was sought after as an ingredient of gunpowder and for making fuses, because of its even, slow-burning properties. It remained in use until after the Second World War. The berries and bark when fresh cause vomiting, but a drug extracted from the dried bark can be used safely as a purgative. Natural dyes in shades of yellow or brown come from the bark, while the fruit yields green or bluish-grey dyes. Butchers used to favour its hard, easily sharpened wood for skewers, and some trees are still cut for pea or bean sticks.

Alder buckthorn is not related to the alder, although they are often seen together and their leaves bear a superficial resemblance. Nor does it have thorns, although some other buckthorns have them. An alternative name is black dogwood, because the butcher's spikes and skewers made from it were once called 'dogs'. Its hanging yellow leaves and purple berries make it particularly attractive in autumn. While it is usually seen around marshes, alder buckthorn also occurs as a shrub layer in open, deciduous woodland such as the New Forest.

The shiny leaves are alternate and untoothed, with 7–9 pairs of parallel veins. Greenish flowers appear in early summer at the junctions of leaves and twigs. Bark is smooth and black.

The branches ascend, the lowest from ground level, to form a bushy outline up to 15 ft (4·5 m) high.

Location

Date

Habitat

Sketches

Caterpillars of the green hairstreak butterfly feed on the leaves.

This tall deciduous shrub sends out suckers freely to form dense thickets. It can grow to 13 ft (4 m).

The round, bitter, black berries grow in clusters, ripening in August or September.

Leaves are opposite, hairy on both sides and pointed, with veins curving towards the tip. Greenish-white flowers appear in June. Their unpleasant smell is attractive to insects.

The blood-red shoots and crimson colouring of the leaves in late autumn, give this species the Latin name *sanguinea*.

Dogwood *Cornus sanguinea*

From medieval times until early this century, butchers used 'dogs', or skewers, made from the hard, white wood of this native shrub to hold cuts of meat in shape. Dogwood was also used to make goads for beasts of burden, and to burn for making charcoal; a 17th-century account talks of the wood as a source of 'Mill-Cogs, Pestles, Bobins and Spokes for Wheels'.

The shrub is inconspicuous for most of the year but proclaims its presence in autumn with its red leaves and black fruit. It usually occurs in chalk and limestone soils, often invading abandoned pasture land. It spreads both by suckers from the parent plant and by seeds dropped by birds.

The bitter and inedible berries that grow on dogwood were once used as a source of lamp oil; their oily consistency led the Welsh country folk to call dogwood the 'wax tree'. It was also known as the 'dog-tree' or 'dogberry' because its fruit was not even fit for dogs. With the wide variety of uses to which its timber and berries were put, dogwood has played a prominent part in British country life. This was reflected by Shakespeare when he gave the name of Dogberry to the character of the comic constable in *Much Ado About Nothing*.

Location	Sketches
Date	
Habitat	

Male
catkins

Female
catkin

Male and female catkins grow
on separate trees. Male catkins
are grey at first, turning yellow
when ripe with pollen; females
are greenish-white. [Actual sizes]

Leaves are alternate and
short pointed, edged with
small teeth, dark grey-green
on top and woolly beneath.

Tree in
winter.

Female catkins turn
into fruits, green at first
then breaking up into
woolly seeds.

A small, many-stemmed
shrubby tree, which grows
to 50 ft (15 m) high.

Goat willow *Salix caprea*

Goat willow comes into the public eye once a year when its golden, male catkins are used to decorate churches on Palm Sunday. The female catkins are less spectacular, but their smooth, silky surface has gained the tree its popular name of 'pussy willow'. Often the branches gathered for indoor decoration are not true goat willow, but come either from the closely related sallow or from one of the numerous natural crosses between goat willow and other species.

Goat willow flowers early and provides the bees with both pollen and nectar when few flowers are out. The tree is also pollinated by wind. It reproduces easily from seed and colonises waste ground, particularly in damp places, where it flourishes in woodland, scrub and hedges.

The bark contains tannin and, like that of other willows, the drug salicin which is used in medicines. The wood is very soft, the sapwood yellowish-white and the heartwood brown. Although little used now, the light wood was once made into clothes pegs, rake teeth and hatchet handles. A pendulous variety of goat willow found on the banks of the river Ayr in 1840 is cultivated in gardens as the Kilmarnock willow.

Location	Sketches
Date	
Habitat	

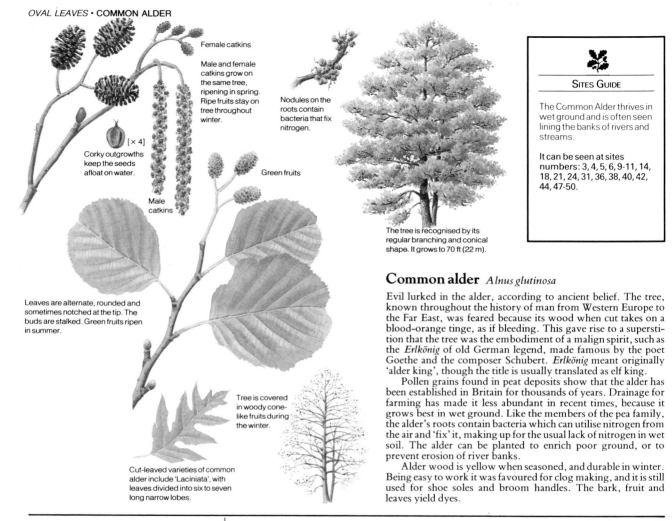

Female catkins

Male and female catkins grow on the same tree, ripening in spring. Ripe fruits stay on tree throughout winter.

Nodules on the roots contain bacteria that fix nitrogen.

[× 4]

Corky outgrowths keep the seeds afloat on water.

Green fruits

Male catkins

Leaves are alternate, rounded and sometimes notched at the tip. The buds are stalked. Green fruits ripen in summer.

Tree is covered in woody cone-like fruits during the winter.

Cut-leaved varieties of common alder include 'Laciniata', with leaves divided into six to seven long narrow lobes.

The tree is recognised by its regular branching and conical shape. It grows to 70 ft (22 m).

Sites Guide

The Common Alder thrives in wet ground and is often seen lining the banks of rivers and streams.

It can be seen at sites numbers: 3, 4, 5, 6, 9-11, 14, 18, 21, 24, 31, 36, 38, 40, 42, 44, 47-50.

Common alder *Alnus glutinosa*

Evil lurked in the alder, according to ancient belief. The tree, known throughout the history of man from Western Europe to the Far East, was feared because its wood when cut takes on a blood-orange tinge, as if bleeding. This gave rise to a superstition that the tree was the embodiment of a malign spirit, such as the *Erlkönig* of old German legend, made famous by the poet Goethe and the composer Schubert. *Erlkönig* meant originally 'alder king', though the title is usually translated as elf king.

Pollen grains found in peat deposits show that the alder has been established in Britain for thousands of years. Drainage for farming has made it less abundant in recent times, because it grows best in wet ground. Like the members of the pea family, the alder's roots contain bacteria which can utilise nitrogen from the air and 'fix' it, making up for the usual lack of nitrogen in wet soil. The alder can be planted to enrich poor ground, or to prevent erosion of river banks.

Alder wood is yellow when seasoned, and durable in winter. Being easy to work it was favoured for clog making, and it is still used for shoe soles and broom handles. The bark, fruit and leaves yield dyes.

Location

Date

Habitat

Sketches

Male catkins

Male and female catkins, borne on the same tree, ripen in early spring. Males are long, females smaller and egg shaped.

Female catkins develop into green fruit.

Grey alder is a broad, rather cone-shaped tree reaching about 80 ft (24 m) in height.

Female catkins

Fruits mature in autumn and hang on tree all winter.

Tree in winter.

Leaves are alternate and pointed, and edged with small teeth on bigger teeth. They are light, dull green on top, grey and hairy beneath.

Grey alder *Alnus incana*

An ugly slag heap can be transformed into a hilly copse within a few years by the planting of grey alder. One of the few trees that will flourish on so loose and infertile a site, it suckers freely and binds the heap together. It has another outstanding virtue: its ability to fix nitrogen from the air increases the fertility of poor soil. Because of this, it has been planted in British woodlands as a 'nurse', helping more demanding trees to grow.

The grey alder is not a native of Britain, but was introduced in 1780 from the Continent, where it grows widely in mountainous areas from Scandinavia to the Alps, and as far east as the Caucasus. It grows naturally by streams, and its numerous suckers bind the gravel beds and protect them from being washed away by flood water.

In Britain too, the grey alder flourishes in cold and wet places, where it is often planted as an ornamental tree. It is also planted on motorway verges, and in the wake of bulldozers on earth-shifting projects. Easily propagated by seeds or cuttings, it unfortunately produces poor quality wood of little commercial value. Several distinct varieties of the tree have been developed, including 'Aurea', which has reddish catkins.

Location

Date

Habitat

Sketches

Hazel nuts are a favourite food of squirrels and mice. Pigeons, jays and pheasants also eat them.

Leaves are alternate, with sawtooth edges, a drawn-out tip and hairy surfaces. They grow to 4 in. (10 cm) long and broad, with a variable outline. Nuts grow in clusters of up to four, each partly enclosed in leafy, overlapping bracts.

Many stems rise from the 'stool' of a coppiced hazel, which if uncut can reach 30 ft (9 m).

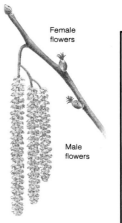

Female flowers

Male flowers

Male flowers hang in 'lambstail' catkins; female flowers appear as tiny buds with protruding red tassels.

SITES GUIDE

Common Hazel grows throughout Britain, and is especially striking in February, when it is covered with catkins.

It can be seen at sites numbers: 9, 14, 18, 22, 26, 36, 38, 40, 48, 49.

Common hazel *Corylus avellana*

Since prehistoric times, pliant hazel rods have been woven into a variety of products useful to man. The primitive coracle, used by Welsh fishermen for 3,000 years, has a basket-like frame of hazel covered by a skin of stretched animal hides or, today, of canvas. Panels of interwoven hazel rods were used in the building technique known as 'wattle and daub': the hazel panels, or wattles, were placed between the wooden posts forming the frame of the house and then daubed with a mixture of mud and straw. Similar woven panels, undaubed, are still used as hurdles to pen sheep, and hazel rods are used in basketwork.

To ensure a steady supply of rods, hazel bushes were 'coppiced' – that is, cut back to ground level at regular intervals, usually of seven years. Where the rods were required for house-building, the hazels were sometimes grown together with tall oaks that would provide the timber for the main frames.

Both hazel rods and the living bushes are used for hedging in country districts. The rods are woven between thorns, which have their main stems partly broken and 'laid' or bent over, giving added strength to the hedge. Alternatively, hazel bushes may be planted and laid to form a dense living barrier.

Location

Date

Habitat

Sketches

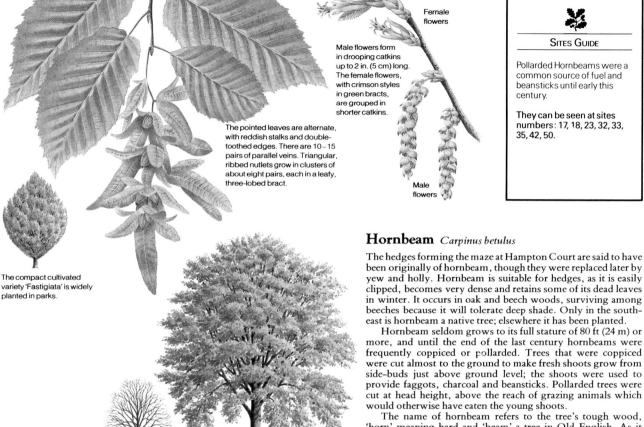

Female flowers

Male flowers form in drooping catkins up to 2 in. (5 cm) long. The female flowers, with crimson styles in green bracts, are grouped in shorter catkins.

The pointed leaves are alternate, with reddish stalks and double-toothed edges. There are 10–15 pairs of parallel veins. Triangular, ribbed nutlets grow in clusters of about eight pairs, each in a leafy, three-lobed bract.

Male flowers

The compact cultivated variety 'Fastigiata' is widely planted in parks.

Steeply rising branches form a rounded crown, up to 80 ft (24 m) high.

SITES GUIDE

Pollarded Hornbeams were a common source of fuel and beansticks until early this century.

They can be seen at sites numbers: 17, 18, 23, 32, 33, 35, 42, 50.

Hornbeam *Carpinus betulus*

The hedges forming the maze at Hampton Court are said to have been originally of hornbeam, though they were replaced later by yew and holly. Hornbeam is suitable for hedges, as it is easily clipped, becomes very dense and retains some of its dead leaves in winter. It occurs in oak and beech woods, surviving among beeches because it will tolerate deep shade. Only in the south-east is hornbeam a native tree; elsewhere it has been planted.

Hornbeam seldom grows to its full stature of 80 ft (24 m) or more, and until the end of the last century hornbeams were frequently coppiced or pollarded. Trees that were coppiced were cut almost to the ground to make fresh shoots grow from side-buds just above ground level; the shoots were used to provide faggots, charcoal and beansticks. Pollarded trees were cut at head height, above the reach of grazing animals which would otherwise have eaten the young shoots.

The name of hornbeam refers to the tree's tough wood, 'horn' meaning hard and 'beam' a tree in Old English. As it resists heavy blows the wood is used for making butchers' chopping blocks, mallets, balls and skittles. Before the days of cheap steel it was fashioned into spokes and cogwheels.

Location	Sketches
Date	
Habitat	

Thrushes feast on the firethorn's berries; blackbirds also find them good eating.

Leaves are alternate with small, regular teeth, dark green and glossy above; thorns bear leaves, and leaf-stalks are hairy. Berries are bright red.

Firethorn is a thorny, evergreen bush, growing in gardens to 5 ft (1·5 m).

Dense heads of white flowers appear in late May and June.

The 'Lalandei' cultivar is widely grown for its big, orange-red berries.

Sites Guide

Firethorn or *Pyracantha* occurs naturally in hedges and thickets; it is also common in gardens, favoured for its flowers and bright shiny berries that last all winter.

Firethorn *Pyracantha coccinea*

Despite its highly evocative common name, firethorn is a shrub that gardeners invariably call by its scientific name of *Pyracantha*. A native of southern Europe, where it occurs naturally in hedges and thickets, *Pyracantha coccinea* was introduced to Britain in the 17th century for the glow of bright red berries which it displays so conspicuously in the autumn. Nowadays the most popular form is the 'Lalandei' cultivar, with orange-red berries. Other species, mostly from China, have also been introduced, some with bright yellow or orange-yellow berries.

Firethorn is particularly suitable for the small garden. Grown as a free-standing bush, it requires no pruning and forms an effective screen; but more frequently it is trained along a wall, where it contrasts happily with red brick or white stone.

The shrub is reproduced by seeds or cuttings and will grow well in most kinds of soil, whether in sun or shade. It tolerates exposure to wind and the atmospheric pollution of cities. It does not, however, like to be moved once established, so it should be transplanted only when young; and although it will accept trimming, it will not bear so many berries for several seasons if it has been pruned to shape.

Location	Sketches
Date	
Habitat	

Ornamental forms of common beech include the narrow, upright-branched 'Dawyck' beech, and the copper beech, or 'Purpurea', with its reddish-purple leaves.

Autumn leaves turn yellow at first, then orange or red-brown.

Female flower

Leaves are alternate, shiny green on both surfaces, with a wavy margin and six to seven pairs of parallel veins.

Male flowers

In a four-valved husk are two triangular nutlets. [Actual size]

Young leaves appear with yellow, long-stalked male flowers and greenish-white female flowers.

Older trees have a massive, many-branched dome; young trees are slimmer and more conical in outline. They grow to about 120 ft (36 m).

SITES GUIDE

The mature Beech creates a thick canopy overhead, casting dense shade which prevents the growth of plants beneath it.

It can be seen at sites numbers: 1-21, 23-25, 27-29, 31, 33-34, 36-37, 39-44, 47-51.

Common beech *Fagus sylvatica*

In the village of Meikleour, near Perth, can be seen a magnificent beech hedge more than two centuries old; it is almost 100 ft (30 m) high, and 600 yds (550 m) long. The story goes that while it was being planted in 1745, the men downed tools on hearing that Bonnie Prince Charlie had landed, and did not return for a year. Afterwards it was left to grow, and it has flourished to become a famous landmark. Less ambitious but still impressive beech hedges are quite common: the tree can be clipped closely and remains dense because it tolerates shade. It thrives in a wide variety of soils, and many ornamental varieties are grown.

Beech wood bends beautifully and can be turned easily, making it an ideal material for furniture, particularly chairs. It is fine-grained and knot-free, the branches falling off early to leave a clean bole. Furthermore its light red-brown colour with darker flecks polishes to a superb natural finish.

Beech chairs have been made in the Chilterns for centuries, and the woodlands there are managed to supply this still-thriving industry. The chairmakers – or 'bodgers' – once worked within the woods, setting up primitive lathes to turn the legs. Factory-made chairs still use traditional designs.

Location

Date

Habitat

Sketches

Female flower

Male flowers

Fruit opens into four valves, releasing its nutlets in September. At about the same time the leaves turn yellow or red.

Leaves are alternate, dark green on top and paler beneath, with 7–11 pairs of parallel veins; they have an unequal base. Male flowers are single and consist of many stamens; female flowers are small and nut-shaped, at base of leaf.

The tall roble beech has an open crown and arching branches. It grows to 75 ft (23 m).

Roble beech *Nothofagus obliqua*

When Spanish explorers reached the areas of South America where this tree grows, its shape reminded them of the oaks they had left behind in Spain, so they called it *roble*, which means oak in Spanish. In fact roble beech is one of several species of *Nothofagus*, or 'false beech', which occur in the Southern Hemisphere. They are also known as southern beeches; some are evergreen and others, like the roble, are deciduous.

Like the other southern beeches, roble once formed extensive forests in South America and especially in Chile, from which country the tree was introduced into Britain in 1903. It is a vigorous, fast-growing tree, frequently growing at the rate of 5–6 ft (1·5–1·8 m) a year. It does not like lime-rich soils, and requires space in which to grow.

The timber of the roble beech, dull reddish-brown in colour, is like that of common beech and is used for similar purposes. It appears to be one of the few hardwoods whose bark is not stripped by the grey squirrel, a menace which makes the growing of hardwood for timber almost impossible in some parts of southern Britain. If this immunity continues, the tree will have increasing value as a source of timber.

Location

Date

Habitat

Sketches

Male flowers

Female flower

Leaves are alternate and prominently ridged between the veins, of which there are 15–18 pairs. The leaf margin is finely toothed, and the stalk is green. Female flowers are small, green and nut-shaped, at base of leaf; male flowers consist of many stamens.

The fruit, dark green then turning brown, resembles a small beech nut. The leaves turn red, gold or pink.

SITES GUIDE

This fast-growing beech from Chile has been planted as an ornamental tree in parks, especially in western Britain and Ireland.

It can be seen at sites numbers: 51, 63.

The tree is conical in profile, with dense foliage. In young trees the branches reach steeply upwards. The raoul grows to 45 ft (14 m).

Raoul *Nothofagus procera*

Under the name *rauli*, the timber of the raoul – like the roble, a form of southern beech – is commercially the most important hardwood in Chile, and natural forests containing the tree have been plundered throughout South America. Generally, the forests have not been replanted; the cleared ground has been used for food crops which give a quicker cash return.

The timber is cherry-coloured, like a redder version of the wood of the common beech, and is fairly dense. It is easy to season, and gives a smooth finish when worked in any direction. It is used to make furniture, floors, doors and stairs.

Both the raoul and the roble beech are being studied by forestry experts in Britain with a view to planting in this country. The raoul grows well here although, since it likes a moist soil, it is best suited to rainier western districts. Once established, it grows quickly, but the buds open early and are susceptible to frost damage in cold springs. Some small stands of raoul are already established as timber trees in British forests, but the species has so far been planted mainly as an ornamental tree in gardens and parks. Its foliage turns from green to rich shades of gold, crimson and pink in autumn.

Location

Date

Habitat

Sketches

Crimson flowers tinge the boughs in spring before the leaves appear.

Winged fruits turn brown when ripe, and fall in July.

Leaves are alternate, about 3 in. (7·5 cm) long, and rough on upper surface. Edge is double-toothed and tip rounded. Base is unequal and does not overlap the stem. Stalk and midrib are hairy.

The single seed is set nearer to the notched tip of fruit than that of the wych elm. [Actual size]

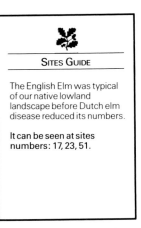

SITES GUIDE

The English Elm was typical of our native lowland landscape before Dutch elm disease reduced its numbers.

It can be seen at sites numbers: 17, 23, 51.

Dutch elm disease is borne by the scolytid beetle, which burrows under the bark and spreads a fungus that blocks the tree's sap.

This tall, narrow-crowned tree, with billowing foliage, grows to 120 ft (36 m).

English elm *Ulmus procera*

Long regarded as one of the traditional sights of hedgerows in the Midlands and southern England, the English elm is a prime example of the way in which man has influenced the landscape. For elms, though probably native trees, were comparatively rare until the 17th and 18th centuries, when great landowners planted them at intervals along the hedges used to enclose farm land, and landscape gardeners introduced them as ornamental trees to beautify their parklands.

Ironically, in establishing the elm as one of our most familiar trees, man was also responsible for its susceptibility to disease. To meet the demand for a stately looking tree that retained its leaves until well into the autumn, nurseries propagated a few such strains by taking the suckers that sprang up around the roots of selected trees. All Britain's elms are therefore genetically similar, and any disease to which they have little resistance can spread unchecked.

Dutch elm disease, so called because it was first identified in Holland, entered the country in 1967 and has destroyed one in five of the timber trees of our hedgerows, more than 12 million English elms being the principal victims.

Location

Date

Habitat

Sketches

Leaves turn a distinctive yellow in autumn.

Purplish flowers appear before leaves.

Leaves are alternate, about 6 in. (15 cm) long, hairy on top and below. Edge is double-toothed and tip long and pointed. Base is unequal and sometimes covers short, stout stalk. Winged fruits fall in July.

Seed is larger than that of English elm, and set in centre of fruit. [Actual size]

Sites Guide

Wych Elm occurs mainly in the north and east of Britain, generally in hilly country. It is often found beside water.

It can be seen at sites numbers: 3, 6, 9, 10, 22, 26, 30, 40, 44, 46, 47, 50-52.

Wych elm is broader than English elm but grows to only 100 ft (30 m) high.

Wych elm *Ulmus glabra*

Hardiest of the many species of elm, the wych elm grows further north than other elms and can flourish even on hillsides and near the sea, and in polluted atmospheres. It is unlike most elms also in reproducing itself by seed, and not by suckers from the roots of the parent tree; this means of propagation has given wych elm a greater resistance to Dutch elm disease. The name 'wych' comes from an Anglo-Saxon word meaning pliable, and refers to the tree's twigs. It used to be thought good luck for a horseman to carry a riding-switch cut from an elm tree.

The heartwood of wych elm is an attractive reddish-brown, with an occasional green streak, and the sapwood broad and yellow. Elm wood is extremely tough, and has many uses. Because it is durable, even in perpetually wet conditions, elm was much used in the past for underground water pipes, which were made by hollowing out entire tree trunks with an auger.

Today, elm is used for the keels of boats, for groynes and for harbour works. Being almost impossible to split, elm is also the ideal wood for the seats of chairs and the hubs of wooden wheels, into which legs and spokes have to be firmly driven. Elm also provides the traditional wood used for coffins.

Location

Date

Habitat

Sketches

Flowers mature into winged seeds.

Leaves are alternate, with double-toothed edges and a sharply pointed tip. They are bright green and shiny on top; the stalk is hairy. The base of the leaf has one side rounded and the other straight.

Seed is near notch in tip of wing, as in English elm. [Actual size]

SITES GUIDE

The flat fields of the east Midlands and East Anglia are the setting for most of England's Smooth-leaved Elms.

They can be seen at site number: 50.

Wheatley elm

Ulmus carpinifolia var. *sarniensis*

The leaves of this variety are darker and rounder. Its compact crown and vertical branches make it especially suitable for avenues and street planting.

This narrow tree has branches ascending from the trunk, then turning down at the ends. It grows to a height of about 90 ft (27 m).

Smooth-leaved elm *Ulmus carpinifolia*

Preferring warmer climates than other elms, the smooth-leaved elm occurs in Britain only in southern and eastern counties. On the Continent, however, it used to be as familiar a sight as the English elm was in England, before the ravages of Dutch elm disease greatly reduced the numbers of both species. Like the English elm, the smooth-leaved elm produces suckers from around the base of the trunk. Unlike the English elm, however, the smooth-leaved elm does not rely entirely on these suckers as a means of propagation, for it also produces fertile seeds.

In East Anglia the smooth-leaved elm is pollarded, or cut off at about head-height, to produce a crop of shoots which are used as peasticks. More commonly seen than the smooth-leaved elm itself are two tall, narrow varieties of it that are often planted as ornamental trees. These are the Cornish elm and the Wheatley, or Jersey, elm. Developed in coastal regions, both varieties are tolerant of salty winds, and so are useful for forming windbreaks near the sea.

A rarer form is the lock elm, which occurs in the Midlands and East Anglia; the name refers to its timber, which is so hard to saw or plane that the tools become 'locked' into the wood.

Location	Sketches
Date	
Habitat	

The leaves of Huntingdon elm (*Ulmus × hollandica* 'Vegeta') are about 4 in. (10 cm) long, with a double-toothed edge and lop-sided base. They are smooth and shiny on top, with hairy tufts in the axils beneath.

SITES GUIDE

Huntingdon Elm is one of several hybrids in the Dutch Elm group. It is often planted in parks. Virtually all these trees have been destroyed by elm disease.

Commelin elm
Ulmus × hollandica 'Commelin'

The leaves of this variety are smaller than those of Huntingdon elm.

All Dutch elms have ascending branches and fairly narrow crowns, growing to 100 ft (30 m).

Dutch elm *Ulmus × hollandica*

Dutch elms are natural hybrids between the smooth-leaved elm and the wych elm, both of which occur together on the Continent. Most of these hybrids are vigorous and have characters intermediate between those of the parents.

The varieties of Dutch elm most commonly planted as street trees are Huntingdon elm, called after the nursery in Huntingdon where they were first raised in this country, and Commelin elm, bred in Holland in an attempt to produce a strain resistant to Dutch elm disease. Unfortunately this was not wholly successful, and no elm with complete immunity has yet been grown.

All elms have a reputation for shedding their branches without warning, and big boughs occasionally crash to the ground, particularly when there has been a long season of drought. This characteristic gave rise long ago to the saying: 'Ellum hateth man and waiteth'. Boy Scouts are often warned not to pitch their tents under elms.

The wood of Dutch elm is like that of wych elm, and has similar uses. It is particularly suitable for interior work, as it warps less than other elm wood.

Location

Date

Habitat

Sketches

The numerous, solitary white flowers appear Feb.–Mar., before the leaves come out.

Leaves are alternate, glossy green on top and hairless. The leaf margin has small, regular, round-ended teeth. Fruits, pale green in summer, turn the colour of ripe tomatoes.

The purple-leaved cherry plum, *atropurpurea* or 'Pissardii', is grown in suburban gardens.

This spreading, open-crowned tree resembles blackthorn, but it blooms earlier, and its foliage is not so thick. It grows to 25 ft (7·5 m).

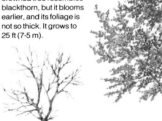

Cherry plum *Prunus cerasifera*

The pure white flowers of the cherry plum splash hedgerow and garden by the beginning of March, heralding the spring before winter is properly over. Because it spreads freely by suckering, the tree is useful for forming dense hedges, and its thorny twigs make it an effective barrier. Its common name describes its cherry-like fruits; the alternative name of myrobalan plum is thought to come from Greek words meaning a fruit producing a sweet-scented ointment.

Like other members of the prunus family, the cherry plum was cultivated for its fruits before being replaced by more rewarding fruit trees. It is one of the parents from which cultivated plums and gages have arisen, and such trees are often grafted on to its rootstock.

The cherry plum is probably best known in the form of the purple-leaved cultivar 'Pissardii'. This was named after Pissard, French-born gardener to the Shah of Persia in the late 19th century. It arose by chance in the Imperial gardens and Pissard cultivated it, and sent specimens to France. It is now grown extensively in suburban gardens for its decorative foliage, and for the pinkish flowers it produces in early spring.

Location	Sketches
Date	
Habitat	

White flowers distinguish pears from apple trees.

Leaves are dark, glossy green, with smaller teeth than apple and a longer leaf-stalk. Fruits ripen from yellow-green to brown.

Pear is narrow, with sparse branches, and often leans; it grows to 50 ft (15 m). Suckers may form a thicket round the parent.

All cultivated pears are derived from the common pear, which itself is probably of hybrid origin.

'Williams' Bon Chrétien'

'Conference'

Common pear *Pyrus communis*

Unlike the crab apple, the common or wild pear is not thought to be native to Britain; it is more likely to have escaped from orchards, to which it had been brought from Continental Europe. Originally, the common pear came from western Asia, but its fruit has been eaten in Europe for thousands of years. It was cultivated by the ancient Greeks, and is mentioned by Homer in the *Odyssey*.

In its wild state, the common pear is a thorny tree with bitter and gritty fruit. It sends out suckers freely from its roots, multiplying to form thickets distinguished by the snowfall of white blossom which covers them in April. The wood is a pale pink-brown in colour, easily stained and polished and used for musical instruments, carving, turning and veneers.

The wild pear is used as a root stock on which are grafted the many cultivated orchard varieties of the tree, which provide dessert pears, fruit for stewing, and perry, a cider-like drink probably introduced by the Normans. Like apples, pear trees often have mistletoe growing on them. Birds leave the sticky seeds on the bark, where the mistletoe develops as a parasite, drawing its sustenance partly from the host tree.

Location

Date

Habitat

Sketches

Creamy-white flowers appear in May and are sweet-scented.

The berries, green at first, ripen to bright scarlet and provide food for birds.

Leaves are alternate, with a white felt of thick hairs on the underside. Each leaf has 9–12 pairs of parallel veins and is irregularly toothed.

Whitebeam is a compact, domed tree with few upswept branches, growing to 80 ft (24 m).

Sites Guide

Silvery-white leaves, emerging in spring, make the Whitebeam appear to be covered in blossom, before its flowers emerge.

It can be seen at sites numbers: 9, 17, 21, 30, 44, 50 and 51.

Whitebeam *Sorbus aria*

The hard, tough wood of the whitebeam was used for making cogs in early machinery, before it was replaced by iron. Over-ripe whitebeam berries were made into a jelly for eating with venison. Although both these uses are largely things of the past, the whitebeam has found an important new function as a decorative street tree. The whitebeam's compact shape and relatively modest size allow it to be planted in restricted spaces; and the hairy undersides of its leaves resist pollution and sea winds and help the tree to conserve moisture on dry sites. In addition, for most of the year the whitebeam is strikingly handsome. From spring onwards, the white down beneath the leaves decks the tree in silver, until red berries and golden leaves bring a new array of colours in the autumn.

The Anglo-Saxons, who gave the tree its name ('beam' meant tree, like *Baum* in modern German), used it as a boundary marker because of its distinctive appearance. In its natural state it grows on dry limestone and chalk soils, a number of different forms growing in various parts of the country. It also hybridises with other members of its family and has been developed into numerous varieties by human intervention.

Location

Date

Habitat

Sketches

Leaves are alternate, and hairy on both sides. They are smaller than plum leaves. The small, round, purple fruit has a waxy bloom.

SITES GUIDE

The Damson has long been cultivated for its small, plum-like fruits which ripen during September and October. Although not a woodland tree, it may be found growing on its own near a house or farm.

The white flowers, which open Apr. – May, are pollinated by insects.

Plum and greengage are larger-fruited than the damson, but all are varieties of *Prunus domestica*.

The damson is a small tree not reaching more than 20–25 ft (6–7·5 m) in height.

Damson *Prunus domestica*

The damson gets its name from the city of Damascus in Syria where, according to tradition, it was first cultivated. Many major food plants were developed in the Middle East, some of the more important, such as corn, evolving into superior forms by the crossing of species and doubling of the chromosomes. When this happens the resulting plant is very vigorous and much larger than its parents. Such doubling has occurred with plums.

Like the greengage and the plum, the damson has been developed from crosses between the blackthorn and the cherry plum. In Britain it is seldom cultivated in orchards, occurring more frequently as a single tree near a house or farm. It spreads easily, either by suckering or by germinating from the stones dropped by people and birds after eating the fruit.

Unlike most fruit trees, the damson does not need pruning to produce a good crop every year. Its fruit can be stewed, bottled, jellied or made into jam. The wood of all plum trees has a reddish heartwood and pale brown sapwood; it is hard and dense, taking polish well. Because of the attractive colour contrast between heartwood and sapwood, damson is used for turning and cabinet-making.

Location

Date

Habitat

Sketches

Flowers are all
alike and fertile.
[× 2]

The oval berries, borne in
a flat head, are red at first,
then ripen to a shiny black.

SITES GUIDE

The colourful berries of the
Wayfaring Tree often brighten
the edges of woods or
hedgerows.

Leaves are opposite,
with dense, white hairs
on the underside. The
edges have regular,
pointed teeth; the stalks
are hairy. Unlike those of
the related guelder rose,
all flowers making up the
flower-head are the same size.

This small, spreading shrub seldom
rises to more than 20 ft (6 m).

Wayfaring tree *Viburnum lantana*

The 16th-century botanist John Gerard found this shrub so
widespread along lanes and byways in southern England that he
called it the 'wayfarer's tree'. The shrub usually grows on the
edges of woods and in hedgerows on chalk and limestone soils,
and does not occur naturally further north than Yorkshire.

Wayfaring tree is a corruption of wayfarer's tree, but the
shrub has a still older name – hoarwithy. 'Hoar', meaning
white, refers to the white, silky hairs on the underside of the
leaves, which reduce water loss on dry soils; and 'withy' means a
pliant stem. The young twigs are so flexible that they were used
to bind faggots in the days before string. They were also cut to
make switches for driving livestock. In the past the black berries
were used to make ink, and the very hard wood from the tree
stem was fashioned into mouthpieces for tobacco-pipes.

The wayfaring tree provides a bright splash of white when it
flowers in May and June. Its red berries, turning black with
maturity, are also attractive in appearance. To human taste they
are so astringent as to be inedible. Birds like them, however, and
spread the seeds on to nearby pastures, which are readily invaded by seedlings or suckers when fields are abandoned.

Location	Sketches
Date	
Habitat	

White flowers in May and rich red autumn leaves make the Snowy Mespil a decorative tree for much of the year.

Leaves are alternate, toothed and with a short point at the tip. They are pink when unfolding in April.

The round, sweet fruit is red at first, turning purple when it ripens in June. [Actual size]

The snowy mespil may grow to 40 ft (12 m). It usually has several stems, but is sometimes pruned back to one.

Snowy mespil produces profuse quantities of white flowers with strap-shaped petals.

Snowy mespil *Amelanchier laevis*

Mespil is derived from the Latin word for medlar, a once-popular apple-like fruit that is edible only when it is partly rotten. Mespil fruits resemble small medlars, but are sweeter-tasting. The Red Indians of North America gathered and dried them for winter eating, and they can be used in puddings and pies or made into jam. The word 'snowy' refers to the brilliant white flowers which appear in May and whose nectar is particularly attractive to bees and wasps. Snowy mespil is sometimes confused with the related shrub *Amelanchier canadensis*; this has young leaves that are woolly on both sides, whereas those of snowy mespil are smooth. Both have rich autumn colours.

Mespils grow well in Britain on light, acid soils and are hardy so long as they are planted where they receive plenty of sunlight. Their rootstock is often used for the grafting of pears and quinces. The wood is heavy, strong and close-grained, the heartwood is dark brown tinged with red, and the sapwood is lighter. The wood is used to make tool handles and fishing rods.

In their native North America the trees are sometimes called June berries, shad berries or shad blow, because they flower and fruit when shad – a migrating fish – are present in the rivers.

Location

Date

Habitat

Sketches

45

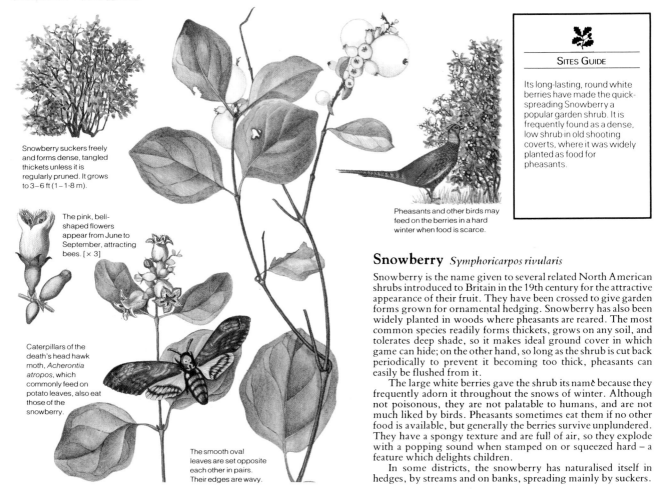

Snowberry suckers freely and forms dense, tangled thickets unless it is regularly pruned. It grows to 3–6 ft (1–1·8 m).

The pink, bell-shaped flowers appear from June to September, attracting bees. [× 3]

Caterpillars of the death's head hawk moth, *Acherontia atropos*, which commonly feed on potato leaves, also eat those of the snowberry.

The smooth oval leaves are set opposite each other in pairs. Their edges are wavy.

Pheasants and other birds may feed on the berries in a hard winter when food is scarce.

Snowberry *Symphoricarpos rivularis*

Snowberry is the name given to several related North American shrubs introduced to Britain in the 19th century for the attractive appearance of their fruit. They have been crossed to give garden forms grown for ornamental hedging. Snowberry has also been widely planted in woods where pheasants are reared. The most common species readily forms thickets, grows on any soil, and tolerates deep shade, so it makes ideal ground cover in which game can hide; on the other hand, so long as the shrub is cut back periodically to prevent it becoming too thick, pheasants can easily be flushed from it.

The large white berries gave the shrub its name because they frequently adorn it throughout the snows of winter. Although not poisonous, they are not palatable to humans, and are not much liked by birds. Pheasants sometimes eat them if no other food is available, but generally the berries survive unplundered. They have a spongy texture and are full of air, so they explode with a popping sound when stamped on or squeezed hard – a feature which delights children.

In some districts, the snowberry has naturalised itself in hedges, by streams and on banks, spreading mainly by suckers.

Location	Sketches
Date	
Habitat	

The leaves are alternate, unlobed and untoothed with tapered base and short-pointed tip; they are dark on top and paler below, often dusted with red.

The long capsule contains many small, flattened seeds. [Actual size]

The purple flowers appear in May and June in clusters of 10–15. They are 2 in. (5 cm) across.

SITES GUIDE

A native of Asia Minor, the Rhododendron now grows wild in many parts of Britain, often shading out other plants. It forms impenetrable thickets on acid, peaty soils.

Rhododendron *Rhododendron ponticum*

When the rhododendron was introduced to the British Isles from Asia Minor more than 200 years ago, it was extensively planted for game cover in woods. It was chosen for this purpose because it adapts to all kinds of soils and situations, and can survive under the heavy shade of beech trees. In some areas it now forms a dense and almost impenetrable shrub layer beneath the trees. It spreads freely by seed and is very difficult to eradicate, either by cutting or with the use of weed-killers.

Along with the cherry laurel, rhododendron is the most common evergreen to have been introduced to Britain. Some of the earlier ornamental rhododendrons were obtained by crossing *Rhododendron ponticum* with other hardy species from the Himalayas and China. It is still used as rootstock on which to graft the hundreds of cultivars and hybrids now in existence. These provide a wide range of colour, flowering from early spring until well into summer.

Although the shrub enjoys the sun, rapid warming-up damages the beautiful flowers, as they need time to thaw out slowly on frosty mornings. Ideally therefore, the shrub should be planted in sheltered places.

Among hundreds of cultivated species of rhododendrons and azaleas is *Rhododendron luteum*, a deciduous form with smaller, yellow flowers.

This evergreen shrub, with dark green, glossy foliage, grows to 20 ft (6 m) high. It spreads rapidly and smothers all other growth in its vicinity.

Location	Sketches
Date	
Habitat	

47

Erect heads of dull, white flowers are borne in the leaf axils in April. [× 3]

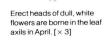

SITES GUIDE

Cherry Laurel is tolerant of shade and when growing wild forms dense cover for game and many forms of wildlife.

The round berries are red at first, ripening to shiny black. [Actual size]

The alternate, bright green glossy leaves are leathery and pointed. They have small, wavy teeth and thick stalks. When crushed, the leaves smell of almonds.

This evergreen grows to 20 ft (6 m) and spreads to form hedges.

Cherry laurel *Prunus laurocerasus*

When the cherry laurel, a native of south-east Europe, was introduced into this country in 1576 it immediately found favour as an ornamental evergreen hedge. The laurel hedge which is such a familiar feature of suburban gardens is in fact cherry laurel and not a true laurel. It is hardy, and grows on most soils except those which contain chalk.

This shrub is, apart from the rhododendron, the most common introduced evergreen in Britain. It is planted as game cover in woods because it can tolerate shade and the moisture dripping from the trees above, and its large evergreen leaves keep the ground warm in winter for game birds. In such shady situations it does not flower or fruit well, but as a hedge it freely produces flowers and cherry-like fruit, which when ripe are eaten by birds.

In the days when amateur naturalists made collections of butterflies, the leaves of cherry laurel formed part of their simple equipment. The leaves smell of bitter almonds when crushed and contain prussic acid or cyanide; butterflies dropped into a 'killing jar' containing the crushed leaves quickly died, but remained relaxed enough to be pinned out.

Location

Date

Habitat

Sketches

The flower is creamy-white, waxy and fragrant with a hawthorn-like scent. There are about 20 five-petalled flowers on each stalk; only a few develop into berries. [× 5]

The hanging berries are at first red, turning later to purplish-black.

SITES GUIDE

This native of Spain and Portugal is widely grown in Britain for its ornamental flowers and evergreen foliage. Although not a woodland shrub, it may well be seen growing in game coverts where it is planted for the protection it affords to pheasants.

This laurel has dense foliage; it usually develops a rounded shrubby profile, but can reach 20 ft (6 m) in height.

The alternate leaves are on red stalks; they are dark glossy green on top and yellow-green below, with many teeth and long, pointed tips. Long, drooping flower spikes appear in June.

Portugal laurel *Prunus lusitanica*

The main distinguishing feature of the Portugal laurel is the dark crimson colour of its twigs and leaf-stalks. It is a native of Spain and Portugal, and was introduced to Britain as an ornamental plant in 1648. Together with cherry laurel and holly, it was then one of the few evergreens available for planting.

Portugal laurel is much hardier than cherry laurel, and unlike cherry laurel it can grow in chalky areas. However, it is not so frequently planted. Where it is planted it is usually grown as a hedge, but if it is given plenty of room and allowed to grow naturally it forms a beautiful ornamental tree. Portugal laurel can also be grown in tubs for decoration, and is kept within bounds by clipping. Unlike the other laurels it has not become naturalised in Britain.

Because it is easily controlled, the plant is often grown in game coverts, where it acts as a windbreak between other trees and keeps the wood warm in winter. It also suppresses the growth of ground plants beneath it, which allows the pheasants to move about freely without becoming trapped. As it often grows into a small tree, pheasants can roost in its branches away from foxes and other predators.

Location	Sketches
Date	
Habitat	

A rounded, bushy shrub, growing to 12 ft (3·6 m) high. It is hardy and evergreen.

Shiny, dark green, leathery leaves are opposite and often have yellow spots. They have a pointed tip, few teeth, a prominent midrib and a long stalk.

The round berries are green at first, ripening to scarlet in the following spring. Each has a single seed. The berries are not usually eaten by birds.

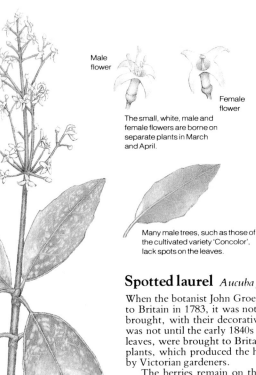

Male flower

Female flower

The small, white, male and female flowers are borne on separate plants in March and April.

Many male trees, such as those of the cultivated variety 'Concolor', lack spots on the leaves.

SITES GUIDE

This native of Japan tolerates dense shade, and grows in corners of gardens where little else will thrive. It may also spread to woodland.

Spotted laurel *Aucuba japonica*

When the botanist John Groefer introduced this native of Japan to Britain in 1783, it was not realised that all the plants he had brought, with their decorative spotted leaves, were female. It was not until the early 1840s that male plants, with pure green leaves, were brought to Britain. They then fertilised the female plants, which produced the handsome scarlet berries favoured by Victorian gardeners.

The berries remain on the shrub throughout the autumn, winter and spring, adding to the ornamental effect of its foliage. At one time spotted laurel was a popular house-plant, while out of doors it became a favourite for planting in banks with other ornamental shrubs and trees alongside garden paths.

The spotted laurel is still popular today, and many different forms of male and female bushes, with variously coloured leaves, have been developed. Since it does not demand much light, it is a very suitable plant for filling in the dark corners of shrubberies or planting under dense trees; it will make a thick hedge to obscure unsightly buildings. It tolerates the polluted air of industrial Britain, and will thrive on almost any soil, however poor. In some areas it now grows wild.

Location

Date

Habitat

Sketches

Birds feed on
the bright red
cherries in July.

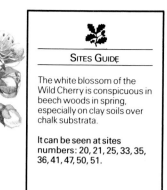

[Actual size]

Leaf turns
crimson in
autumn.

The white flowers
of wild cherry
appear before the
leaves in April.

Leaves are alternate, with
long points and regular,
forward-pointing teeth.
There are glands at the
base, and the stalk is
red and grooved.

The tree is pyramidal in shape,
reaching 30–40 ft (9–12 m).

Wild cherry *Prunus avium*

The cherry, like other fruit trees, has been crossed and selected
to produce better fruiting varieties. Many of these derive from
the wild cherry, or gean, which is still used as the rootstock on
which its more productive relatives are grown. The wild cherry
can be found in woods – especially beech woods – where its
blossoms stand out in snow-white patches in spring.

Wild cherry grows rapidly to timber size, and its wood is
used to make fine furniture, veneers and sweet-smoking cherry
pipes. The wood is of good quality, though larger trees sometimes suffer from heart rot.

The 'cherry ripe' of the old London street cry came from the
cultivated varieties of the tree grown in Kent, where farmers
grazed their sheep beneath the trees, making double use of the
land. Harvesting the fruit was once a social occasion: on cherry-
picking Sunday in Cambridgeshire a century ago, a small pay-
ment enabled people to eat as many cherries as they could
manage in a day. The fruit is now eaten fresh or prepared in a
variety of ways, and is also used in syrups and cough mixtures.
Liqueurs are distilled from the fermented pulp, with which the
stones are also crushed.

Location	Sketches
Date	
Habitat	

The black cherries, called 'hags' in Scotland, are taken by birds, though they have a bitter taste. They contain a hard, oval stone.

The bird cherry is usually smaller than the wild cherry, reaching about 20–30 ft (6–9 m).

The sickly, almond-scented white flowers hang in long spikes in May. The light green leaves are leathery with fine, regular teeth.

Bird cherry *Prunus padus*

Few trees can match the outstanding beauty of the bird cherry's display in May, when long, hanging bunches of blossom fill the air with an almond fragrance. As the tree's name implies, however, its bitter fruit is edible only to birds. Its bark, though, was once used by humans: in the Middle Ages it was the source of an infusion used as a tonic and as a sedative for upset stomachs, while pieces of the bark were hung outside doors and put in drinking water as a guard against plague.

The tart taste of the cherry is due to its richness in tannin, and the fruit itself has its uses – to flavour brandies and wines. A very similar species, the black or rum cherry, is used for flavouring rum. Timber from the tree has a reddish-brown heartwood and white sapwood, and gives off a somewhat disagreeable smell.

Bird cherry is often planted as an ornamental tree: a number of cultivars have bigger and more varied flowers – white, pink and double. One of them, 'Watereri', has spectacular hanging blossoms. Bird cherries are found much farther north than the wild cherry, and have a variety of local names, among them 'hag cherry', 'hawkberry' or 'hagberry' in Scotland and Northumberland, from the tree's old Norse name *heggr*.

Location

Date

Habitat

Sketches

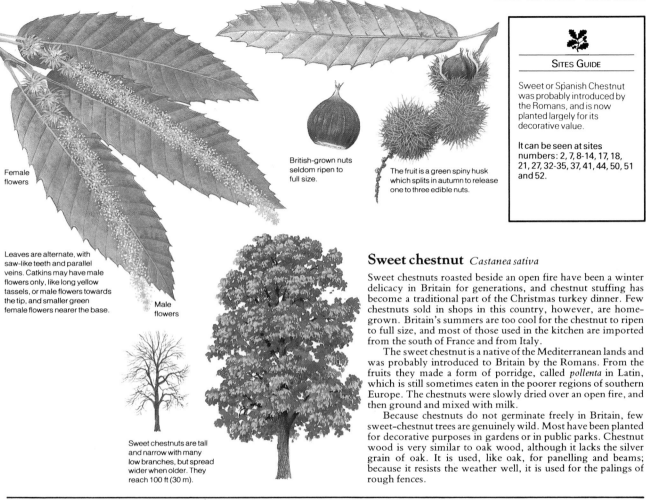

Female flowers

British-grown nuts seldom ripen to full size.

The fruit is a green spiny husk which splits in autumn to release one to three edible nuts.

Leaves are alternate, with saw-like teeth and parallel veins. Catkins may have male flowers only, like long yellow tassels, or male flowers towards the tip, and smaller green female flowers nearer the base.

Male flowers

Sweet chestnuts are tall and narrow with many low branches, but spread wider when older. They reach 100 ft (30 m).

Sweet chestnut *Castanea sativa*

Sweet chestnuts roasted beside an open fire have been a winter delicacy in Britain for generations, and chestnut stuffing has become a traditional part of the Christmas turkey dinner. Few chestnuts sold in shops in this country, however, are home-grown. Britain's summers are too cool for the chestnut to ripen to full size, and most of those used in the kitchen are imported from the south of France and from Italy.

The sweet chestnut is a native of the Mediterranean lands and was probably introduced to Britain by the Romans. From the fruits they made a form of porridge, called *pollenta* in Latin, which is still sometimes eaten in the poorer regions of southern Europe. The chestnuts were slowly dried over an open fire, and then ground and mixed with milk.

Because chestnuts do not germinate freely in Britain, few sweet–chestnut trees are genuinely wild. Most have been planted for decorative purposes in gardens or in public parks. Chestnut wood is very similar to oak wood, although it lacks the silver grain of oak. It is used, like oak, for panelling and beams; because it resists the weather well, it is used for the palings of rough fences.

Location

Date

Habitat

Sketches

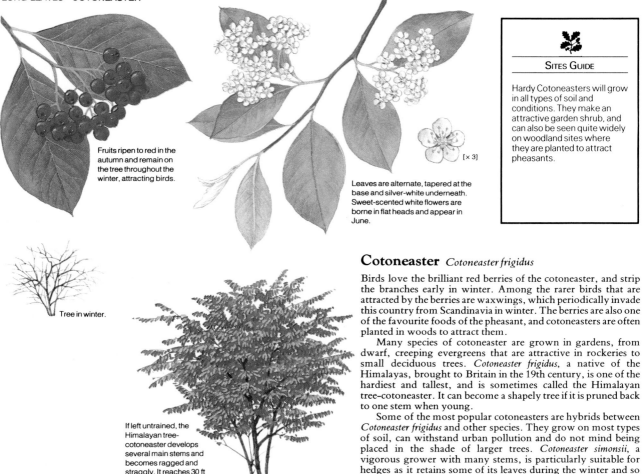

Fruits ripen to red in the autumn and remain on the tree throughout the winter, attracting birds.

[× 3]

Leaves are alternate, tapered at the base and silver-white underneath. Sweet-scented white flowers are borne in flat heads and appear in June.

Tree in winter.

If left untrained, the Himalayan tree-cotoneaster develops several main stems and becomes ragged and straggly. It reaches 30 ft (9 m) in height.

Cotoneaster *Cotoneaster frigidus*

Birds love the brilliant red berries of the cotoneaster, and strip the branches early in winter. Among the rarer birds that are attracted by the berries are waxwings, which periodically invade this country from Scandinavia in winter. The berries are also one of the favourite foods of the pheasant, and cotoneasters are often planted in woods to attract them.

Many species of cotoneaster are grown in gardens, from dwarf, creeping evergreens that are attractive in rockeries to small deciduous trees. *Cotoneaster frigidus*, a native of the Himalayas, brought to Britain in the 19th century, is one of the hardiest and tallest, and is sometimes called the Himalayan tree-cotoneaster. It can become a shapely tree if it is pruned back to one stem when young.

Some of the most popular cotoneasters are hybrids between *Cotoneaster frigidus* and other species. They grow on most types of soil, can withstand urban pollution and do not mind being placed in the shade of larger trees. *Cotoneaster simonsii*, a vigorous grower with many stems, is particularly suitable for hedges as it retains some of its leaves during the winter and so remains decorative throughout the year.

Location

Date

Habitat

Sketches

[Actual size]

The fruits are four-lobed seed capsules, which turn a deep pinkish-red when ripe. They are matt, not glossy, and contain four orange-coloured seeds.

[× 2]

The light green leaves are opposite, thin and pointed, with small teeth. The small, greenish-yellow flowers have narrow petals.

Spindle *Euonymus europaeus*

The white, hard and dense wood of this small tree was used from ancient times for making spindles. The 'spinsters', usually un-married girls, held the raw wool in one hand and rotated it on to the spindle with the other; the rotation kept the wool fibres tight and helped draw the loose wool into a thread. A round, flattish stone with a hole in the middle – a spindle whorl – was threaded over the end of the spindle to act as a primitive fly-wheel and keep the spindle turning – a device improved upon by the spinning wheel. The wood of the spindle was also known as skewerwood and pegwood, indicating its other uses; and today it makes high-quality charcoal for artists.

For most of the year the spindle is an inconspicuous shrub, but in the autumn it declares its identity with a display of dark red leaves and pinkish-red, four-lobed fruits. Because of its autumn show, the spindle is cultivated in gardens and parks as a decorative tree, and some attractive varieties have been de-veloped.

The tree has an unpleasant smell if bruised and the fruit is an emetic. In former times the powdered leaves and seeds were dusted on the skin of children and animals to drive away lice.

Spindle is a small tree or big bush reaching 20 ft (6 m) in woods and hedgerows. Cultivated forms occur in parks. The tree does particularly well on chalk soils.

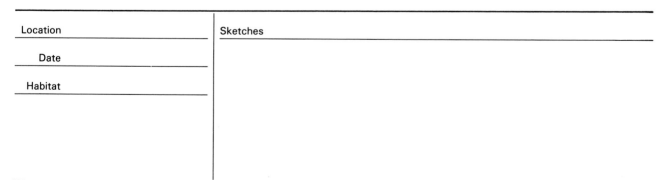

Location	Sketches
Date	
Habitat	

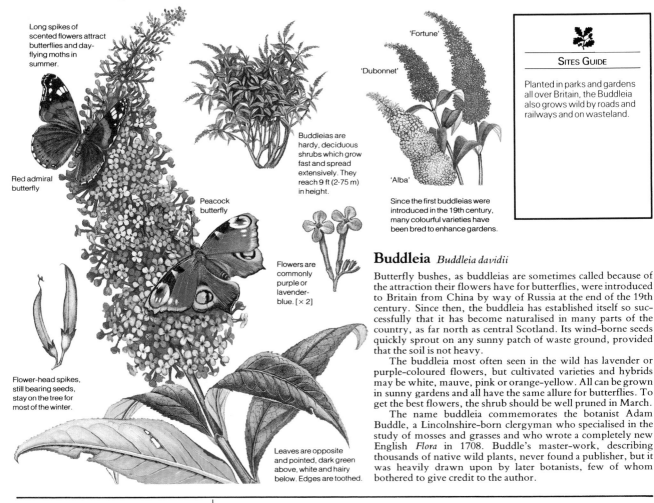

Long spikes of scented flowers attract butterflies and day-flying moths in summer.

Red admiral butterfly

Buddleias are hardy, deciduous shrubs which grow fast and spread extensively. They reach 9 ft (2·75 m) in height.

Peacock butterfly

Flowers are commonly purple or lavender-blue. [× 2]

Flower-head spikes, still bearing seeds, stay on the tree for most of the winter.

Leaves are opposite and pointed, dark green above, white and hairy below. Edges are toothed.

'Fortune'

'Dubonnet'

'Alba'

Since the first buddleias were introduced in the 19th century, many colourful varieties have been bred to enhance gardens.

SITES GUIDE

Planted in parks and gardens all over Britain, the Buddleia also grows wild by roads and railways and on wasteland.

Buddleia *Buddleia davidii*

Butterfly bushes, as buddleias are sometimes called because of the attraction their flowers have for butterflies, were introduced to Britain from China by way of Russia at the end of the 19th century. Since then, the buddleia has established itself so successfully that it has become naturalised in many parts of the country, as far north as central Scotland. Its wind-borne seeds quickly sprout on any sunny patch of waste ground, provided that the soil is not heavy.

The buddleia most often seen in the wild has lavender or purple-coloured flowers, but cultivated varieties and hybrids may be white, mauve, pink or orange-yellow. All can be grown in sunny gardens and all have the same allure for butterflies. To get the best flowers, the shrub should be well pruned in March.

The name buddleia commemorates the botanist Adam Buddle, a Lincolnshire-born clergyman who specialised in the study of mosses and grasses and who wrote a completely new English *Flora* in 1708. Buddle's master-work, describing thousands of native wild plants, never found a publisher, but it was heavily drawn upon by later botanists, few of whom bothered to give credit to the author.

Location

Date

Habitat

Sketches

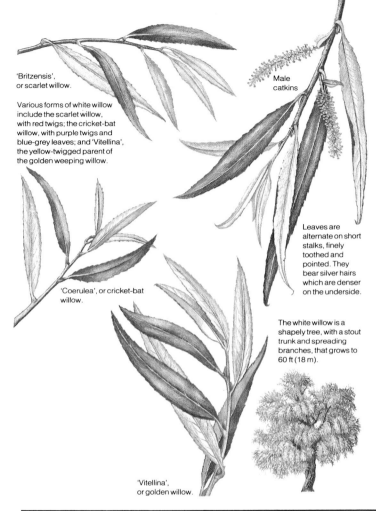

'Britzensis',
or scarlet willow.

Various forms of white willow
include the scarlet willow,
with red twigs; the cricket-bat
willow, with purple twigs and
blue-grey leaves; and 'Vitellina',
the yellow-twigged parent of
the golden weeping willow.

'Coerulea', or cricket-bat
willow.

Male
catkins

Leaves are
alternate on short
stalks, finely
toothed and
pointed. They
bear silver hairs
which are denser
on the underside.

The white willow is a
shapely tree, with a stout
trunk and spreading
branches, that grows to
60 ft (18 m).

'Vitellina',
or golden willow.

Yellow male catkins and
green female catkins form on
separate trees in spring.

Female
catkins

Female catkins ripen to
produce fluffy seeds that are
distributed by the wind.

White willow *Salix alba*

Pollarded willows used to be a frequent sight in the low-lying
regions of England. The practice of pollarding involved cutting
off the tops of the trees at head height, out of reach of grazing
animals, to give a regular crop of small poles suitable for
fencing, basketry or firewood. In modern times, however,
pollarding has declined, and the willows themselves have become scarcer as they are uprooted to make the cleaning of rivers
and ditches by machinery easier.

The decline of the willow may well prove to be to the
eventual detriment of the countryside, for the roots of waterside
trees bind the soil of the banks together and reduce erosion. One
area in which white willows are still commonly seen is East
Anglia, where a cultivated variety is widely grown as a source of
wood for cricket bats.

Cricket-bat willows are planted in rich riverside soil, where
they grow exceptionally fast. They are felled at 12–15 years old,
by which time they may be 60 ft (18 m) tall. The trunk is cut into
'rounds' about 30 in. (76 cm) long, and then divided lengthwise
into triangular segments with a wedge and mallet. Each triangular 'cleft' is then shaped into a bat.

Location

Date

Habitat

Sketches

Green female
catkins appear
in May.

The hairless leaves, often
twisted, are shiny green
on top and grey-green
below.

In summer, female
catkins mature into
white woolly seeds.

Yellow male
catkins are borne
on separate trees
from the female
catkins. The twigs
break off easily.

If allowed to grow to its full height, the
crack willow will reach 80 ft (24 m),
producing a rounded, green crown.

Crack willows are often
pollarded to provide
straight poles for hurdles.

Crack willow *Salix fragilis*

The twigs of this willow are very brittle (*fragilis* in Latin) and can
be snapped off easily; from this characteristic are derived both its
common and botanical names. This brittleness has proved of
great value to the crack willow, as it has allowed it to develop a
peculiar method of spreading far afield. Usually the tree grows
by the side of a river, so many of its broken twigs fall into the
water, to be carried off and lodged in the mud downstream,
where they take root and grow into new trees. This willow does
not, therefore, rely entirely on its seed to reproduce itself. The
seeds stay fertile for only a short time, and require moist soil on
which to germinate soon after they are shed.

Paradoxically, charcoal obtained from willow twigs is less
brittle than other kinds, except perhaps for that made from
spindle, and is therefore preferred by artists for drawing. In
some places the roots of crack willow were once boiled to
produce a purple dye, used at Easter to decorate hens' eggs.

Crack willows play an important role on river banks in
preventing erosion by holding the soil together with their long,
penetrating roots. They tolerate a polluted atmosphere, and can
also grow well in salty air near the coast.

Location

Date

Habitat

Sketches

Leaves are very long and narrow, green on top, with dense, silvery hairs beneath. They are sharp-pointed and without teeth; edges are rolled inwards on the underside.

The common osier is a shrub that has been coppiced to produce many quickly grown shoots; it reaches 33 ft (10 m).

Straight, flexible shoots are felted when young; male and female catkins grow on separate twigs before the leaves.

Leaf margins rolled inwards.

Female flower [× 5]

Male catkin (actual size)

Female catkin (actual size)

Male flower [× 5]

Osier *Salix viminalis*

As this willow is a shrub rather than a tree, it is not pollarded like other willows to produce straight poles. Instead it is coppiced – that is, cut down to ground level once a year, so that the osier grows a mass of long, pliant stems, or 'withies'. These are ideal for basket-work, and in the past there was heavy demand for them in the manufacture of fish-traps, lobster-pots, chairs and countless other objects, including the shopping basket. Even today, commercial withy-growing is still practised in Britain, especially in Somerset, and the willow is still used for remedial therapy and basket-making by blind people.

When the one-year-old shoots are harvested, they are known as green willows. Brown willow is obtained by steaming the osier shoots and then drying them, the bark being left on. To make buff willow the shoots are boiled and the bark is stripped off; it is tannin from the bark that turns the rods their buff shade. White willow can be prepared only in spring, when the sap starts to rise in lengths that have been stored on end in standing water over winter. The bark is then stripped off. A traditional dance known as 'strip the willow' owes its name to the 'peeling-off' sequence of the dancers' movements.

Location

Date

Habitat

Sketches

The long tubed flower contains the male stamens with the female ovary below. [× 4]

The black berries are poisonous to man, but birds can eat them without harm. [× 2]

Small green flowers appear Feb. – Apr. in clusters among upper leaves. They are pollinated by insects.

Leaves are evergreen, up to 4½ in. (12 cm) long and thick, dark and glossy. They taper to the base and are usually clustered near the top of the plant.

Small upright branches, usually bare except at the top, may rise to more than 40 in. (100 cm) in height.

SITES GUIDE

Spurge Laurel, an uncommon though native shrub, thrives on chalky soil and can tolerate deep woodland shade.

Spurge laurel *Daphne laureola*

Dwarfed by oaks, beeches and other woodland companions, this fragile-looking shrub must make the most of its meagre share of sunshine. Evergreen leaves – thick and tough enough to withstand the repeated dripping of rainwater – help it to absorb much of the light it needs for growth at times when deciduous trees are bare. It starts to blossom in winter, before a new canopy of foliage above plunges it into summer-long gloom.

Spurge laurel is neither a spurge nor a laurel, although the flowers recall those of some members of the spurge family and the leaves bear a strong resemblance to laurel leaves. That similarity is borne out in the botanical name, *daphne*. In Greek mythology Daphne was a river nymph who appealed to the gods to help her to resist the advances of Apollo. They turned her into a laurel bush, whereupon he donned the head-wreath of laurel leaves which the Romans later adopted as a symbol of heroism and victory.

Britain has only one other native daphne, the deciduous *Daphne mezerium*, which has pink or red flowers. However, many species from other parts of the world are cultivated in Britain for their fragrance and decorative appearance.

Location

Date

Habitat

Sketches

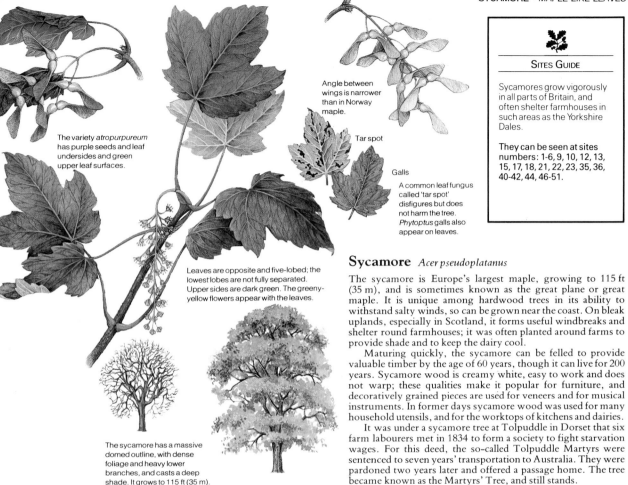

The variety *atropurpureum* has purple seeds and leaf undersides and green upper leaf surfaces.

Angle between wings is narrower than in Norway maple.

Tar spot

Galls

A common leaf fungus called 'tar spot' disfigures but does not harm the tree. *Phytoptus* galls also appear on leaves.

Leaves are opposite and five-lobed; the lowest lobes are not fully separated. Upper sides are dark green. The greeny-yellow flowers appear with the leaves.

The sycamore has a massive domed outline, with dense foliage and heavy lower branches, and casts a deep shade. It grows to 115 ft (35 m).

Sycamore *Acer pseudoplatanus*

The sycamore is Europe's largest maple, growing to 115 ft (35 m), and is sometimes known as the great plane or great maple. It is unique among hardwood trees in its ability to withstand salty winds, so can be grown near the coast. On bleak uplands, especially in Scotland, it forms useful windbreaks and shelter round farmhouses; it was often planted around farms to provide shade and to keep the dairy cool.

Maturing quickly, the sycamore can be felled to provide valuable timber by the age of 60 years, though it can live for 200 years. Sycamore wood is creamy white, easy to work and does not warp; these qualities make it popular for furniture, and decoratively grained pieces are used for veneers and for musical instruments. In former days sycamore wood was used for many household utensils, and for the worktops of kitchens and dairies.

It was under a sycamore tree at Tolpuddle in Dorset that six farm labourers met in 1834 to form a society to fight starvation wages. For this deed, the so-called Tolpuddle Martyrs were sentenced to seven years' transportation to Australia. They were pardoned two years later and offered a passage home. The tree became known as the Martyrs' Tree, and still stands.

Location	Sketches
Date	
Habitat	

In autumn the leaves turn
yellow or scarlet-brown.

The yellow flowers appear
before the leaves.

The thin, light green leaves are
opposite and have long points.
The leaf-stalk is also long.

The Norway maple is a shorter
and more slender tree than the
sycamore, reaching 90 ft (27 m).

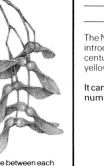

The angle between each
wing of the seed is wider
than in the sycamore.

SITES GUIDE

The Norway Maple,
introduced in the 17th
century, bears clusters of pale
yellow flowers in early spring.

It can be seen at sites
numbers: 2, 17, 29, 50, 51.

Norway maple *Acer platanoides*

Harsh climatic conditions in the mountains of northern continental Europe which are its native home make the Norway
maple very hardy and resistant to frost. It seeds freely, and has
reproduced itself and become naturalised in Britain. In Scotland
it is planted for both shelter and ornament, and in southern
Britain it brightens many city streets and parks. It is suited for
growing in towns because it tolerates smoke and grime. It
thrives on most soils and the leaves, unlike those of some
ornamental maples, do not lose their green colour on soils which
contain lime.

   Yellow clusters of flowers appear in early spring before the
leaves. They provide a useful source of food for bees at a time of
year when little other food is available. There are many ornamental forms of the Norway maple, some with variegated or
purple leaves.

   The young tree grows quickly but is prone to attack by grey
squirrels, which strip off and eat the bark and also the sweet sap
beneath. The wood is of good quality and indistinguishable
from that of the sycamore, but is less useful because, coming
from a smaller tree, it is not available in the larger sizes.

Location

Date

Habitat

Sketches

In autumn, leaf turns amber-yellow.

Leaves are opposite and small, with three main, round-tipped lobes and two smaller basal lobes. In summer they are dull green above, downy below.

Each pair of seed wings lies in an almost straight line. Wings are often tinged with pink.

The small yellow-green flowers form erect clusters. Emerging leaves have a pinkish tinge.

The field maple is a round-headed tree with a sinuous trunk; the ends of its branches droop, then turn up. It grows up to 85 ft (26 m).

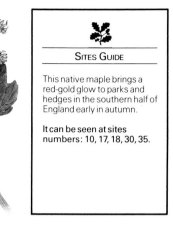

SITES GUIDE

This native maple brings a red-gold glow to parks and hedges in the southern half of England early in autumn.

It can be seen at sites numbers: 10, 17, 18, 30, 35.

Field maple *Acer campestre*

The decorative 'bird's-eye maple', used for furniture veneers and wall panelling, comes from the field maple. The distinctive figured pattern is obtained by cutting across the small knots which form on the trunk. At one time the wood was also used for making domestic utensils, such as drinking bowls.

All the maples produce useful wood, but field maples of timber-producing size have disappeared and not been replaced, as the wood of other maples has become more freely available. Maple wood is used for violin-making and forms the back, sides and neck of the instrument. The rippled grain used for the backs is known as 'fiddle back'. The supreme violin-maker, Antonio Stradivarius (1644–1737), was the first to use a bridge of maple to support the strings. The quality of his instruments owed much to the way in which the wood was seasoned, and to the composition of the finishing varnish.

Usually the field maple is seen only in hedgerows growing in the chalky soils of the southern half of England, and it is often cut back to form a trim hedge. In the past it was used for topiary work. If it is allowed to grow unclipped or is planted as a single tree, it can reach a considerable height.

Location

Date

Habitat

Sketches

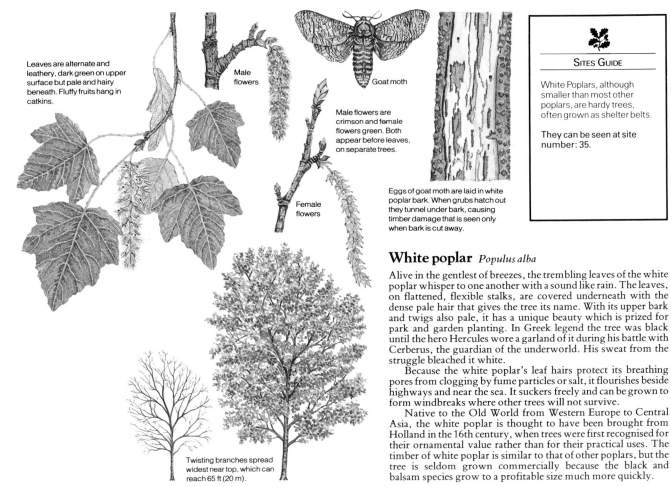

Leaves are alternate and leathery, dark green on upper surface but pale and hairy beneath. Fluffy fruits hang in catkins.

Male flowers

Goat moth

Male flowers are crimson and female flowers green. Both appear before leaves, on separate trees.

Female flowers

Eggs of goat moth are laid in white poplar bark. When grubs hatch out they tunnel under bark, causing timber damage that is seen only when bark is cut away.

Twisting branches spread widest near top, which can reach 65 ft (20 m).

White poplar *Populus alba*

Alive in the gentlest of breezes, the trembling leaves of the white poplar whisper to one another with a sound like rain. The leaves, on flattened, flexible stalks, are covered underneath with the dense pale hair that gives the tree its name. With its upper bark and twigs also pale, it has a unique beauty which is prized for park and garden planting. In Greek legend the tree was black until the hero Hercules wore a garland of it during his battle with Cerberus, the guardian of the underworld. His sweat from the struggle bleached it white.

Because the white poplar's leaf hairs protect its breathing pores from clogging by fume particles or salt, it flourishes beside highways and near the sea. It suckers freely and can be grown to form windbreaks where other trees will not survive.

Native to the Old World from Western Europe to Central Asia, the white poplar is thought to have been brought from Holland in the 16th century, when trees were first recognised for their ornamental value rather than for their practical uses. The timber of white poplar is similar to that of other poplars, but the tree is seldom grown commercially because the black and balsam species grow to a profitable size much more quickly.

Location _____

Date _____

Habitat _____

Sketches

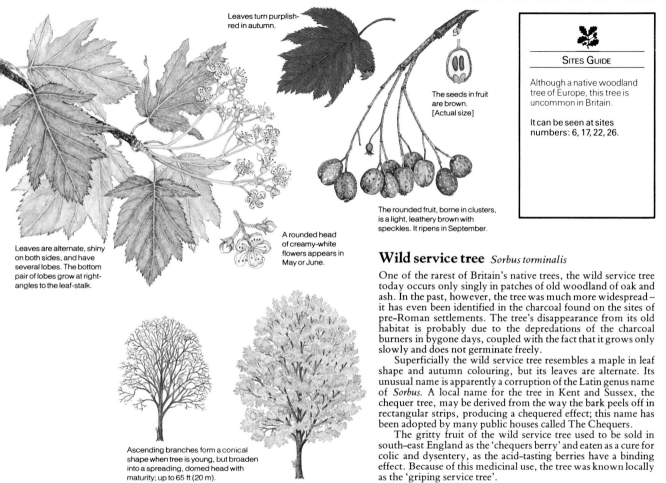

Leaves turn purplish-red in autumn.

The seeds in fruit are brown. [Actual size]

The rounded fruit, borne in clusters, is a light, leathery brown with speckles. It ripens in September.

Leaves are alternate, shiny on both sides, and have several lobes. The bottom pair of lobes grow at right-angles to the leaf-stalk.

A rounded head of creamy-white flowers appears in May or June.

Ascending branches form a conical shape when tree is young, but broaden into a spreading, domed head with maturity; up to 65 ft (20 m).

Wild service tree *Sorbus torminalis*

One of the rarest of Britain's native trees, the wild service tree today occurs only singly in patches of old woodland of oak and ash. In the past, however, the tree was much more widespread – it has even been identified in the charcoal found on the sites of pre-Roman settlements. The tree's disappearance from its old habitat is probably due to the depredations of the charcoal burners in bygone days, coupled with the fact that it grows only slowly and does not germinate freely.

Superficially the wild service tree resembles a maple in leaf shape and autumn colouring, but its leaves are alternate. Its unusual name is apparently a corruption of the Latin genus name of *Sorbus*. A local name for the tree in Kent and Sussex, the chequer tree, may be derived from the way the bark peels off in rectangular strips, producing a chequered effect; this name has been adopted by many public houses called The Chequers.

The gritty fruit of the wild service tree used to be sold in south-east England as the 'chequers berry' and eaten as a cure for colic and dysentery, as the acid-tasting berries have a binding effect. Because of this medicinal use, the tree was known locally as the 'griping service tree'.

Location

Date

Habitat

Sketches

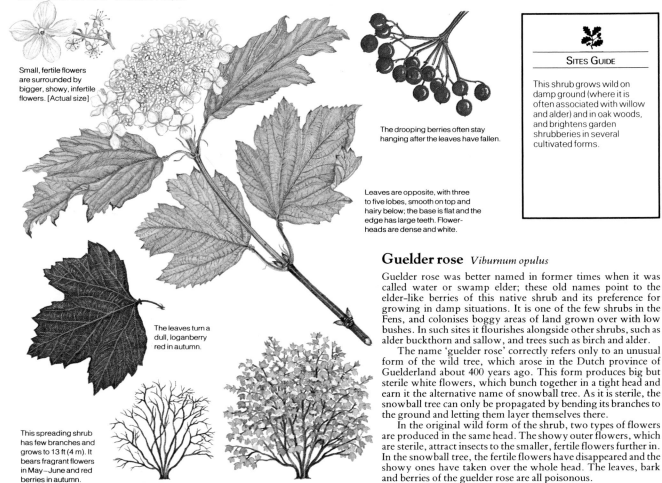

Small, fertile flowers are surrounded by bigger, showy, infertile flowers. [Actual size]

The drooping berries often stay hanging after the leaves have fallen.

Leaves are opposite, with three to five lobes, smooth on top and hairy below; the base is flat and the edge has large teeth. Flower-heads are dense and white.

The leaves turn a dull, loganberry red in autumn.

This spreading shrub has few branches and grows to 13 ft (4 m). It bears fragrant flowers in May–June and red berries in autumn.

Guelder rose *Viburnum opulus*

Guelder rose was better named in former times when it was called water or swamp elder; these old names point to the elder-like berries of this native shrub and its preference for growing in damp situations. It is one of the few shrubs in the Fens, and colonises boggy areas of land grown over with low bushes. In such sites it flourishes alongside other shrubs, such as alder buckthorn and sallow, and trees such as birch and alder.

The name 'guelder rose' correctly refers only to an unusual form of the wild tree, which arose in the Dutch province of Guelderland about 400 years ago. This form produces big but sterile white flowers, which bunch together in a tight head and earn it the alternative name of snowball tree. As it is sterile, the snowball tree can only be propagated by bending its branches to the ground and letting them layer themselves there.

In the original wild form of the shrub, two types of flowers are produced in the same head. The showy outer flowers, which are sterile, attract insects to the smaller, fertile flowers further in. In the snowball tree, the fertile flowers have disappeared and the showy ones have taken over the whole head. The leaves, bark and berries of the guelder rose are all poisonous.

Location	Sketches
Date	
Habitat	

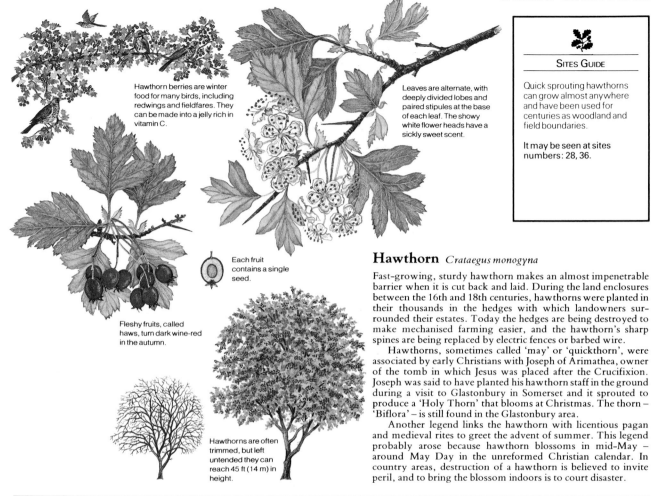

Hawthorn berries are winter food for many birds, including redwings and fieldfares. They can be made into a jelly rich in vitamin C.

Leaves are alternate, with deeply divided lobes and paired stipules at the base of each leaf. The showy white flower heads have a sickly sweet scent.

Each fruit contains a single seed.

Fleshy fruits, called haws, turn dark wine-red in the autumn.

Hawthorns are often trimmed, but left untended they can reach 45 ft (14 m) in height.

SITES GUIDE

Quick sprouting hawthorns can grow almost anywhere and have been used for centuries as woodland and field boundaries.

It may be seen at sites numbers: 28, 36.

Hawthorn *Crataegus monogyna*

Fast-growing, sturdy hawthorn makes an almost impenetrable barrier when it is cut back and laid. During the land enclosures between the 16th and 18th centuries, hawthorns were planted in their thousands in the hedges with which landowners surrounded their estates. Today the hedges are being destroyed to make mechanised farming easier, and the hawthorn's sharp spines are being replaced by electric fences or barbed wire.

Hawthorns, sometimes called 'may' or 'quickthorn', were associated by early Christians with Joseph of Arimathea, owner of the tomb in which Jesus was placed after the Crucifixion. Joseph was said to have planted his hawthorn staff in the ground during a visit to Glastonbury in Somerset and it sprouted to produce a 'Holy Thorn' that blooms at Christmas. The thorn – 'Biflora' – is still found in the Glastonbury area.

Another legend links the hawthorn with licentious pagan and medieval rites to greet the advent of summer. This legend probably arose because hawthorn blossoms in mid-May – around May Day in the unreformed Christian calendar. In country areas, destruction of a hawthorn is believed to invite peril, and to bring the blossom indoors is to court disaster.

Location	Sketches
Date	
Habitat	

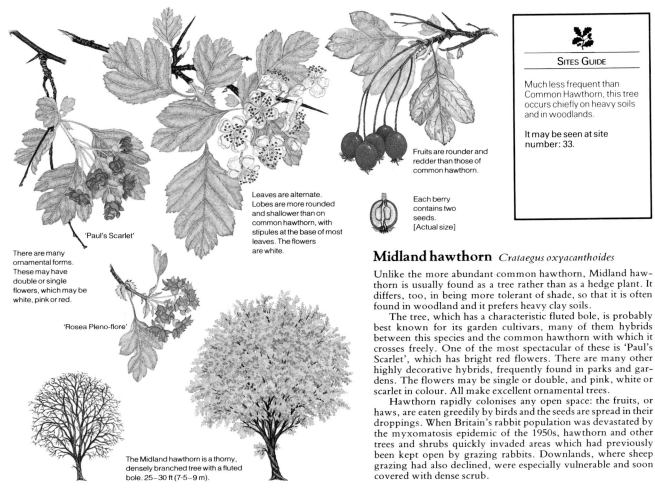

'Paul's Scarlet'

There are many
ornamental forms.
These may have
double or single
flowers, which may be
white, pink or red.

'Rosea Pleno-flore'

The Midland hawthorn is a thorny,
densely branched tree with a fluted
bole. 25–30 ft (7·5–9 m).

Leaves are alternate.
Lobes are more rounded
and shallower than on
common hawthorn, with
stipules at the base of most
leaves. The flowers
are white.

Fruits are rounder and
redder than those of
common hawthorn.

Each berry
contains two
seeds.
[Actual size]

Midland hawthorn *Crataegus oxyacanthoides*

Unlike the more abundant common hawthorn, Midland hawthorn is usually found as a tree rather than as a hedge plant. It
differs, too, in being more tolerant of shade, so that it is often
found in woodland and it prefers heavy clay soils.

The tree, which has a characteristic fluted bole, is probably
best known for its garden cultivars, many of them hybrids
between this species and the common hawthorn with which it
crosses freely. One of the most spectacular of these is 'Paul's
Scarlet', which has bright red flowers. There are many other
highly decorative hybrids, frequently found in parks and gardens. The flowers may be single or double, and pink, white or
scarlet in colour. All make excellent ornamental trees.

Hawthorn rapidly colonises any open space: the fruits, or
haws, are eaten greedily by birds and the seeds are spread in their
droppings. When Britain's rabbit population was devastated by
the myxomatosis epidemic of the 1950s, hawthorn and other
trees and shrubs quickly invaded areas which had previously
been kept open by grazing rabbits. Downlands, where sheep
grazing had also declined, were especially vulnerable and soon
covered with dense scrub.

Location	Sketches
Date	
Habitat	

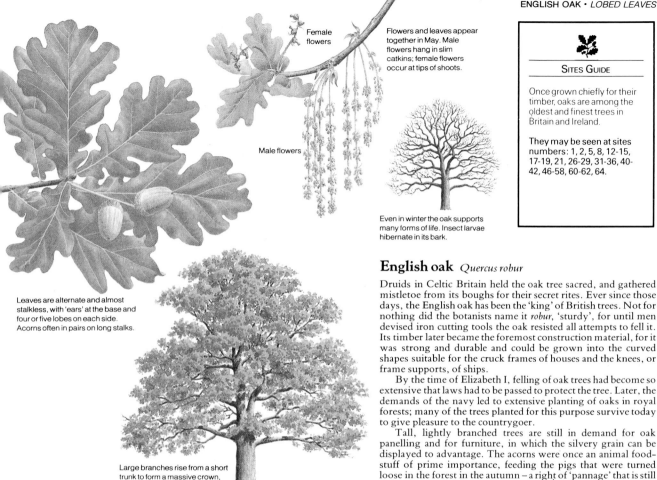

Female flowers

Flowers and leaves appear together in May. Male flowers hang in slim catkins; female flowers occur at tips of shoots.

Male flowers

Even in winter the oak supports many forms of life. Insect larvae hibernate in its bark.

Leaves are alternate and almost stalkless, with 'ears' at the base and four or five lobes on each side. Acorns often in pairs on long stalks.

Large branches rise from a short trunk to form a massive crown, rising to 115 ft (35 m).

Sites Guide

Once grown chiefly for their timber, oaks are among the oldest and finest trees in Britain and Ireland.

They may be seen at sites numbers: 1, 2, 5, 8, 12-15, 17-19, 21, 26-29, 31-36, 40-42, 46-58, 60-62, 64.

English oak *Quercus robur*

Druids in Celtic Britain held the oak tree sacred, and gathered mistletoe from its boughs for their secret rites. Ever since those days, the English oak has been the 'king' of British trees. Not for nothing did the botanists name it *robur*, 'sturdy', for until men devised iron cutting tools the oak resisted all attempts to fell it. Its timber later became the foremost construction material, for it was strong and durable and could be grown into the curved shapes suitable for the cruck frames of houses and the knees, or frame supports, of ships.

By the time of Elizabeth I, felling of oak trees had become so extensive that laws had to be passed to protect the tree. Later, the demands of the navy led to extensive planting of oaks in royal forests; many of the trees planted for this purpose survive today to give pleasure to the countrygoer.

Tall, lightly branched trees are still in demand for oak panelling and for furniture, in which the silvery grain can be displayed to advantage. The acorns were once an animal food-stuff of prime importance, feeding the pigs that were turned loose in the forest in the autumn – a right of 'pannage' that is still jealously guarded by commoners living in the New Forest.

Location

Date

Habitat

Sketches

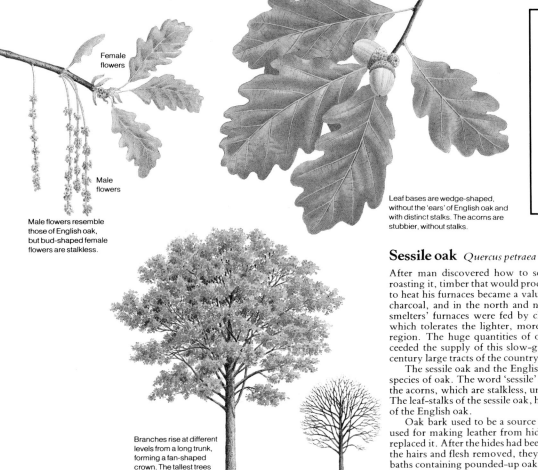

Female flowers

Male flowers

Male flowers resemble those of English oak, but bud-shaped female flowers are stalkless.

Leaf bases are wedge-shaped, without the 'ears' of English oak and with distinct stalks. The acorns are stubbier, without stalks.

Branches rise at different levels from a long trunk, forming a fan-shaped crown. The tallest trees reach 130 ft (40 m).

SITES GUIDE

Sessile Oak is the dominant native oak of the less-fertile, wetter upland regions of Britain and Ireland.

It may be seen at sites numbers: 1, 3-6, 8-10, 22, 24, 34, 37, 39, 40, 44, 50, 53-55, 57, 63.

Sessile oak *Quercus petraea*

After man discovered how to separate iron from its ore by roasting it, timber that would produce steadily burning charcoal to heat his furnaces became a valued crop. Oak made excellent charcoal, and in the north and north-west of Britain the iron smelters' furnaces were fed by charcoal from the sessile oak, which tolerates the lighter, more acid, less-fertile soils of the region. The huge quantities of oak required for charcoal exceeded the supply of this slow-growing tree, and by the 17th century large tracts of the countryside had been denuded.

The sessile oak and the English oak are Britain's two native species of oak. The word 'sessile' means unstalked and refers to the acorns, which are stalkless, unlike those of the English oak. The leaf-stalks of the sessile oak, however, are longer than those of the English oak.

Oak bark used to be a source of tannin, a substance widely used for making leather from hides until man-made chemicals replaced it. After the hides had been softened in a lime pit, and all the hairs and flesh removed, they were passed through tanning baths containing pounded-up oak bark and water. The resultant leather was then rinsed and dried.

Location

Date

Habitat

Sketches

The spiny fruit contains one or more shiny 'conkers' – the nuts of the tree.

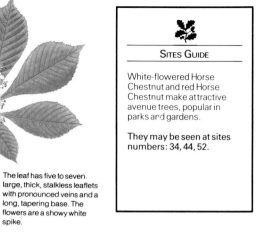

SITES GUIDE

White-flowered Horse Chestnut and red Horse Chestnut make attractive avenue trees, popular in parks and gardens.

They may be seen at sites numbers: 34, 44, 52.

The leaf has five to seven large, thick, stalkless leaflets with pronounced veins and a long, tapering base. The flowers are a showy white spike.

Red horse chestnut
Aesculus × carnea

A common decorative hybrid between horse chestnut and the red buck-eye from North America. Leaves are darker, often smaller; flowers pink or dull red.

Tree in winter.

The horse chestnut, which can attain 115 ft (35 m), has arching branches that are usually turned up at their ends.

Horse chestnut *Aesculus hippocastanum*

Each autumn, schoolboys avidly gather horse chestnuts with which to play conkers. The tree was introduced to Britain from the Balkans in the late 16th century; but it was not until some 200 years later that chestnuts were used for the game. Before that, conkers – the name derives from 'conqueror' – were played with cobnuts or snail shells.

The glossy conkers give the tree its American name of 'buck-eye', as the chestnuts are said to resemble the eye of a deer. Conkers are eaten by deer and cattle, and were sometimes ground up as meal to fatten sheep. There is a tradition that the Turks once fed them to horses to cure broken wind (a respiratory disorder).

Horse chestnuts are often grown as ornamental avenue trees for their 'candles' of flowers, and were frequently planted for this purpose as early as the 17th century. The wood is pale cream or brown; it is very light and weak and of limited economic value. It is used for toys and, being absorbent, for making trays in which to store fruit. Until recently, artificial limbs were made from it, as it is light and easily shaped. The tree grows rapidly on most soils, but requires plenty of space.

Location	Sketches
Date	
Habitat	

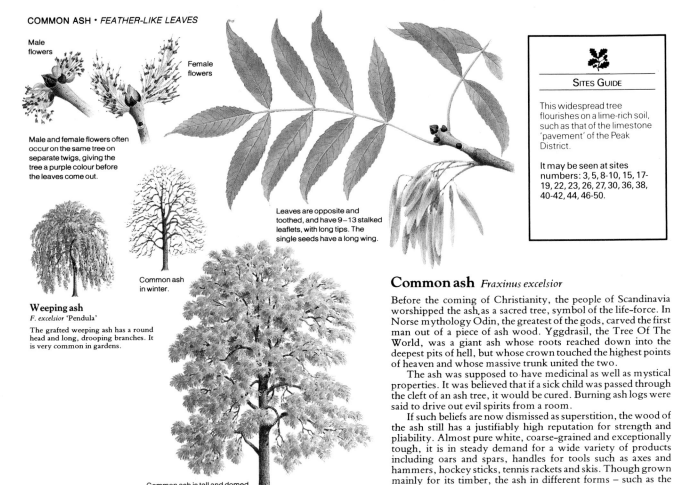

Male flowers

Female flowers

Male and female flowers often occur on the same tree on separate twigs, giving the tree a purple colour before the leaves come out.

Leaves are opposite and toothed, and have 9–13 stalked leaflets, with long tips. The single seeds have a long wing.

Common ash in winter.

Weeping ash
F. excelsior 'Pendula'

The grafted weeping ash has a round head and long, drooping branches. It is very common in gardens.

Common ash is tall and domed with widely spaced branches. It grows to 130 ft (40 m).

SITES GUIDE

This widespread tree flourishes on a lime-rich soil, such as that of the limestone 'pavement' of the Peak District.

It may be seen at sites numbers: 3, 5, 8-10, 15, 17-19, 22, 23, 26, 27, 30, 36, 38, 40-42, 44, 46-50.

Common ash *Fraxinus excelsior*

Before the coming of Christianity, the people of Scandinavia worshipped the ash, as a sacred tree, symbol of the life-force. In Norse mythology Odin, the greatest of the gods, carved the first man out of a piece of ash wood. Yggdrasil, the Tree Of The World, was a giant ash whose roots reached down into the deepest pits of hell, but whose crown touched the highest points of heaven and whose massive trunk united the two.

The ash was supposed to have medicinal as well as mystical properties. It was believed that if a sick child was passed through the cleft of an ash tree, it would be cured. Burning ash logs were said to drive out evil spirits from a room.

If such beliefs are now dismissed as superstition, the wood of the ash still has a justifiably high reputation for strength and pliability. Almost pure white, coarse-grained and exceptionally tough, it is in steady demand for a wide variety of products including oars and spars, handles for tools such as axes and hammers, hockey sticks, tennis rackets and skis. Though grown mainly for its timber, the ash in different forms – such as the weeping ash – is also a popular and versatile ornamental tree. The winged seeds, often called 'keys', grow in bunches.

Location

Date

Habitat

Sketches

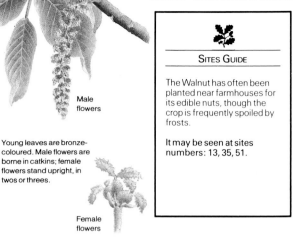

Male flowers

Young leaves are bronze-coloured. Male flowers are borne in catkins; female flowers stand upright, in twos or threes.

Female flowers

The green, rounded fruit contains the familiar crinkled nut with its edible kernel.

The walnut is a handsome, spreading tree with a broad crown and thick bole, reaching 100 ft (30 m).

Each leaf usually has seven leaflets, larger towards the tip. The leaves are set alternately on the twig.

Walnut *Juglans regia*

As the legions of Imperial Rome marched north to conquer the barbarian lands of Gaul and Britain they carried with them the seeds of the walnut tree. The 'royal nut of Jove' was their name for the fruit of the tree, which they prized as a food and as a source of cooking oil.

The walnut, a native of Asia Minor, was imported to Rome from Greece by about 100 BC. The Greeks called it the 'royal nut' or 'Persian nut', names that reflect its importance and its origin, and many of the superstitions and myths about the walnut can be traced back to ancient Greece. The resemblance of the peeled nut to the human brain led to the medieval belief that it could cure mental disorders; this belief arose from the so-called 'doctrine of signatures', according to which preparations made from plants that looked like parts of the human body could be used to treat ailments affecting those parts.

The walnut had many more practical uses. Apart from the value of its timber in furniture making, the oil from the nut was used in the 19th century for soap manufacture, and one horticultural guide of the time, John Loudon's *Suburban Gardener*, recommends a decoction of walnut leaves for killing slugs.

Location	Sketches
Date	
Habitat	

The ripe berries attract birds in autumn. Each leaf has numerous pairs of stalkless leaflets with sharp, forward-pointing teeth.

Creamy-white clusters of flowers form in May.

SITES GUIDE

The Rowan's finest display is in the autumn, with clusters of bright red berries. It flourishes by mountain streams.

It may be seen at sites numbers: 1, 9, 10, 14, 17, 18, 36, 39, 41, 44, 47, 48, 50, 51, 53, 62, 63.

Bastard service tree
Sorbus × thuringiaca

On this tree, the leaf is only partially divided. It is a hybrid of rowan and whitebeam, decorative in streets.

The rowan is a graceful, open tree up to 65 ft (20 m) in height.

Rowan *Sorbus aucuparia*

Connected with witchcraft from ancient times, the rowan tree's name is believed to be derived from the Norse word *runa*, meaning 'a charm'. The tree was often planted outside houses and in churchyards to ward off witches. On May Day, a spray of rowan leaves was hung over doors to repel evil, and wells were dressed with rowan to keep witches away.

The tree's alternative name of mountain ash reflects the fact that it grows higher up mountain-sides than any other native tree, sometimes clinging to a rock face after sprouting in a crevice from seed dropped by a bird. It is widely planted to decorate streets and gardens, not only for its beauty but also because its narrow shape does not take up much room and its sparse foliage allows grass to grow on the ground beneath.

The red berries of rowan are made into a jelly that is eaten with game, and being rich in vitamin C they were once made into a drink to prevent scurvy. Bird-catchers once used the berries as bait for traps to snare thrushes, redwings and fieldfares. The rowan's strong, flexible, yellow-grey wood was once widely used for making tool handles and small carved objects, and was sometimes used instead of yew for making long-bows.

Location

Date

Habitat

Sketches

Flower [Actual size]

The pith inside an elder stalk resembles white, spongy cork.

Autumn berries hang in bunches.

The elder usually remains a bushy shrub, with many stems arising at ground level.

The stalked, toothed leaves are opposite and consist of five to seven leaflets, which smell offensively. The numerous creamy-white flowers form a flat-topped head with a heavy, sweet scent.

If it is given light and space, the elder may grow from a shrub into a small tree up to 30 ft (9 m) tall.

Elder *Sambucus nigra*

Elder flourishes wherever the nitrogen content of the soil is high: near abandoned dwellings, in churchyards and around rabbit warrens and badger setts. In these places the soil has been enriched by the breakdown of organic matter such as dung and refuse. The seeds are spread in the droppings of birds which eat the berries. The plant colonises an area quickly and it soon becomes established, for it grows very vigorously.

Nowadays some cultivars are grown in gardens for their ornamental value, but the tree has been cultivated by man for centuries. The fruits and flowers make excellent wines and jams and are rich in Vitamin C. Coughs were treated with a tea made from the flowers, and an extract of the bark was used as a purgative. Dyes were obtained from different parts of the tree: black from the bark, green from the leaves, and blue or lilac from the flowers.

The pith from the stem is easily cut, and is used for holding botanical specimens while they are sectioned. The wood, which is hard and yellowish-white, makes small items such as toys, combs and wooden spoons. Generations of children have hollowed out the stems to make whistles and peashooters.

Location

Date

Habitat

Sketches

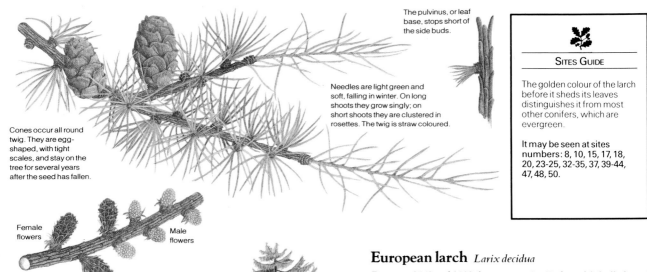

The pulvinus, or leaf base, stops short of the side buds.

Needles are light green and soft, falling in winter. On long shoots they grow singly; on short shoots they are clustered in rosettes. The twig is straw coloured.

Cones occur all round twig. They are egg-shaped, with tight scales, and stay on the tree for several years after the seed has fallen.

Female flowers

Male flowers

Male flowers are yellow and globe-shaped, female flowers loganberry-red with green stripes, in spring.

On a mature tree, the lower stem is clear of branches; the branches higher up are sparse, thick and horizontal. The larch loses its foliage in winter. Grows to 125 ft (38 m).

SITES GUIDE

The golden colour of the larch before it sheds its leaves distinguishes it from most other conifers, which are evergreen.

It may be seen at sites numbers: 8, 10, 15, 17, 18, 20, 23-25, 32-35, 37, 39-44, 47, 48, 50.

European larch *Larix decidua*

Between 1740 and 1830 three successive Dukes of Atholl planted more than 14 million larches on their estates in Perthshire. Until then the larch – which was brought to Britain from central Europe about 1620 – had been grown purely as an ornamental tree. The larches are now part of the natural scenery of the area, forming extensive forests near Dunkeld and Blair Atholl. The tree's high-quality timber with its rust-coloured heartwood is used to make staircases, light furniture, wall panelling and many other products.

On the Continent the larch is a mountain species, adapted to long winters and short growing seasons; in Britain it has a longer growing season, and grows quickly in dry areas. It is vulnerable to spring frost and to numerous diseases, especially larch canker. It needs plenty of light and space in which to flourish; to provide the ideal conditions, larch plantations should be thinned.

As the larch does not cast a heavy shadow and is deciduous, grass and brambles grow beneath it, providing food for sheep in upland areas. The tree is often used in forestry to shelter hardwoods. The fast-growing, short-lived larch is felled and sold, allowing the slow-maturing hardwoods to grow on.

Location

Date

Habitat

Sketches

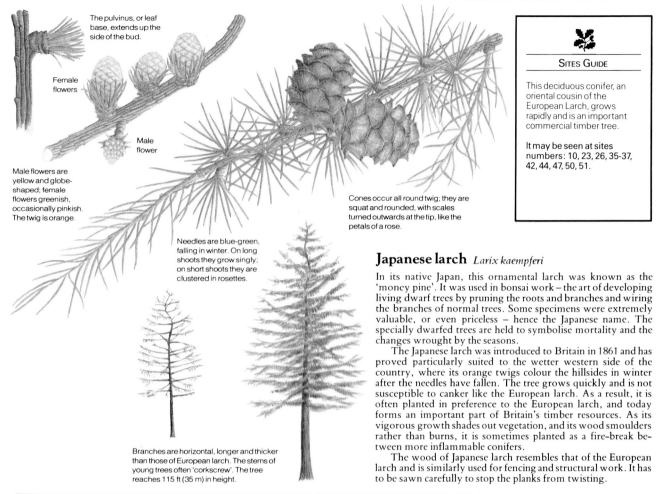

The pulvinus, or leaf base, extends up the side of the bud.

Female flowers

Male flower

Male flowers are yellow and globe-shaped; female flowers greenish, occasionally pinkish. The twig is orange.

Needles are blue-green, falling in winter. On long shoots they grow singly; on short shoots they are clustered in rosettes.

Cones occur all round twig; they are squat and rounded, with scales turned outwards at the tip, like the petals of a rose.

Branches are horizontal, longer and thicker than those of European larch. The stems of young trees often 'corkscrew'. The tree reaches 115 ft (35 m) in height.

Japanese larch *Larix kaempferi*

In its native Japan, this ornamental larch was known as the 'money pine'. It was used in bonsai work – the art of developing living dwarf trees by pruning the roots and branches and wiring the branches of normal trees. Some specimens were extremely valuable, or even priceless – hence the Japanese name. The specially dwarfed trees are held to symbolise mortality and the changes wrought by the seasons.

The Japanese larch was introduced to Britain in 1861 and has proved particularly suited to the wetter western side of the country, where its orange twigs colour the hillsides in winter after the needles have fallen. The tree grows quickly and is not susceptible to canker like the European larch. As a result, it is often planted in preference to the European larch, and today forms an important part of Britain's timber resources. As its vigorous growth shades out vegetation, and its wood smoulders rather than burns, it is sometimes planted as a fire-break between more inflammable conifers.

The wood of Japanese larch resembles that of the European larch and is similarly used for fencing and structural work. It has to be sawn carefully to stop the planks from twisting.

Location

Date

Habitat

Sketches

Male flowers are yellow; female flowers vary from loganberry-red to green. Twig is pinkish, sometimes glaucous, or grey-blue.

Cones are egg-shaped or squat, and the scales are sometimes turned outwards.

Female flowers

Male flowers

Needles vary from light green to blue-green, growing singly on long shoots and in rosettes on short shoots.

The pulvinus, or leaf base, just reaches the base of the bud or short shoot.

This cross between European larch and Japanese larch combines features of both parents. Specimens have so far reached 105 ft (32 m).

Hybrid larch *Larix × eurolepis*

The hybrid or Dunkeld larch, a natural cross between the European larch and the Japanese larch, has in recent years become a tree of major commercial importance in this country. Yet the occurrence of the hybrid came about through nothing more than a fortunate accident.

In 1885, about 20 years after Japanese larch was introduced to Britain, the Duke of Atholl planted 11 specimens of the tree at Dunkeld in Perthshire, to produce seed for planting in his forest nurseries. On the hillside above was some European larch, planted more than 100 years before. It is thought that pollen from these trees drifted down and fertilised flowers on the Japanese larch below, so that when the seed was collected, many of the resultant seedlings were hybrids. These seedlings impressed foresters by their vigorous growth.

The hybrid grows more quickly than either parent. It is now produced deliberately in seed orchards, where selected strains of European and Japanese larch are grafted on to young rootstock. This method encourages the trees to seed early, and also produces small bushy trees from which seed can be more easily collected in large quantities.

Location

Date

Habitat

Sketches

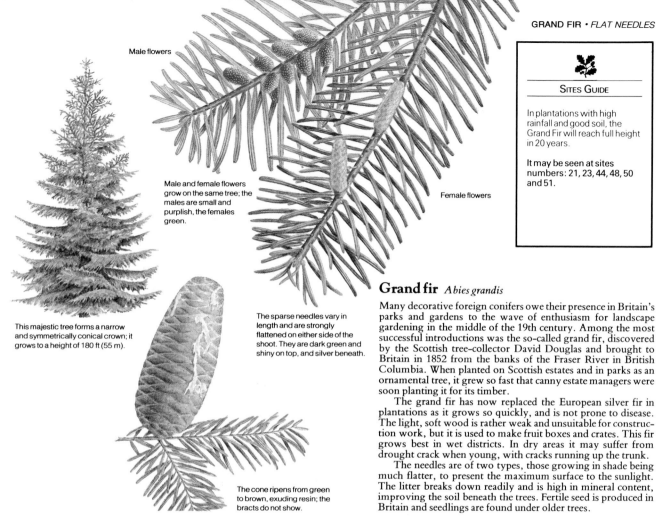

Male flowers

Male and female flowers grow on the same tree; the males are small and purplish, the females green.

Female flowers

This majestic tree forms a narrow and symmetrically conical crown; it grows to a height of 180 ft (55 m).

The sparse needles vary in length and are strongly flattened on either side of the shoot. They are dark green and shiny on top, and silver beneath.

The cone ripens from green to brown, exuding resin; the bracts do not show.

SITES GUIDE

In plantations with high rainfall and good soil, the Grand Fir will reach full height in 20 years.

It may be seen at sites numbers: 21, 23, 44, 48, 50 and 51.

Grand fir *Abies grandis*

Many decorative foreign conifers owe their presence in Britain's parks and gardens to the wave of enthusiasm for landscape gardening in the middle of the 19th century. Among the most successful introductions was the so-called grand fir, discovered by the Scottish tree-collector David Douglas and brought to Britain in 1852 from the banks of the Fraser River in British Columbia. When planted on Scottish estates and in parks as an ornamental tree, it grew so fast that canny estate managers were soon planting it for its timber.

The grand fir has now replaced the European silver fir in plantations as it grows so quickly, and is not prone to disease. The light, soft wood is rather weak and unsuitable for construction work, but it is used to make fruit boxes and crates. This fir grows best in wet districts. In dry areas it may suffer from drought crack when young, with cracks running up the trunk.

The needles are of two types, those growing in shade being much flatter, to present the maximum surface to the sunlight. The litter breaks down readily and is high in mineral content, improving the soil beneath the trees. Fertile seed is produced in Britain and seedlings are found under older trees.

Location		Sketches
Date		
Habitat		

Male flowers

Male flowers are yellow; females are red and shaped like a tassel.

The underside of the leaf has two white bands.

Female flowers

Needles grow all round the shoot, but are parted on the upper and undersides, leaving the shoot exposed.

This very tall, conical tree grows to 180 ft (55 m) in Britain and 325 ft (100 m) in its native North American Rocky Mountains.

[Actual size]

The light-brown cones hang down and have long, protruding bracts, each with three prongs.

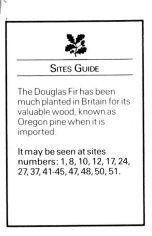

SITES GUIDE

The Douglas Fir has been much planted in Britain for its valuable wood, known as Oregon pine when it is imported.

It may be seen at sites numbers: 1, 8, 10, 12, 17, 24, 27, 37, 41-45, 47, 48, 50, 51.

Douglas fir *Pseudotsuga menziesii*

After the coast redwoods, the Douglas fir is the tallest tree growing on the North American west coast. This magnificent conifer is named after David Douglas, the plant collector who introduced its seeds to Britain in 1827. The newcomer was widely planted at first as a decorative tree, particularly in the policies, or private woodlands, around Scottish mansions. It then began to be grown for commercial purposes, and is now an important timber tree in Britain, and also one of the tallest.

The seed sent by Douglas came from an area with conditions similar to those in Britain. Given good soils, the tree grows well and produces some of Britain's finest timber. On shallow soil it is more prone to disease and may be blown down easily. Douglas firs like plenty of light: too much shade encourages a leaf-sucking aphid, which was unwittingly imported with the tree before the dangers were realised.

Many of Britain's Douglas firs are not yet old enough to produce the first-class timber of North America, where it is called Oregon pine. This is heavy and durable, taking paint and polish well. It is excellent for building work, doors, floors, veneers, and high-quality plywood.

Location

Date

Habitat

Sketches

Mature cone is small and light brown, with a few rounded scales.

Needles part to either side of shoot and vary in length, giving a scattered appearance. They are green on top and white beneath. The shoot is hairy.

SITES GUIDE

The Western Hemlock, which comes from the Pacific seaboard of North America, is grown for ornament and for its wood.

It may be seen at sites numbers: 1, 4, 8, 10, 12, 21, 24, 42-45, 48, 50, 51.

Needles taper to a blunt tip. [× 3]

Down-turned branch tips and shoots, giving the whole tree a drooping appearance, make the western hemlock one of the most attractive conifers. In Britain it grows to 115 ft (35 m).

Western hemlock *Tsuga heterophylla*

The Indians of North America made a kind of bread from the inner bark of the western hemlock, but this magnificent conifer was brought to Britain in the last century for its decorative, not its culinary, value. Discovered by the great horticulturalist David Douglas, who gave his name to the Douglas fir, the western hemlock was planted in gardens and woodlands round large houses on Scottish estates.

A graceful, ornamental tree, the western hemlock can be grown on a wide variety of soils, except those containing chalk. It grows rapidly and regenerates easily, producing many seedlings. It reaches a large size and an age of between 200 and 500 years in its native habitat.

When grown commercially, the amount of timber the tree produces per acre is high, especially in western Britain where moisture is plentiful. The wood has the ability to hold nails well, so is much used for making boxes. As with other hemlocks, the seedlings and young trees require shady, moist conditions, and it is therefore useful for planting under other tree crops. The drooping branch tips prevent the young shoots from being damaged by the branches of the trees under which it is growing.

Location

Date

Habitat

Sketches

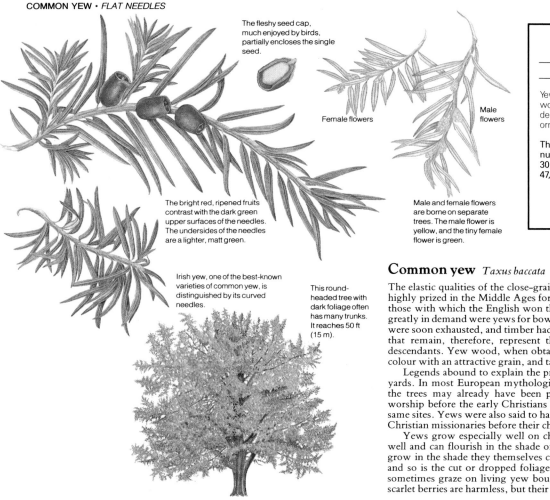

The fleshy seed cap, much enjoyed by birds, partially encloses the single seed.

Female flowers

Male flowers

The bright red, ripened fruits contrast with the dark green upper surfaces of the needles. The undersides of the needles are a lighter, matt green.

Male and female flowers are borne on separate trees. The male flower is yellow, and the tiny female flower is green.

Irish yew, one of the best-known varieties of common yew, is distinguished by its curved needles.

This round-headed tree with dark foliage often has many trunks. It reaches 50 ft (15 m).

SITES GUIDE

Yews are found both wild in woodlands and clipped as decorative hedges in ornamental gardens.

They may be seen at sites numbers: 1, 9, 17-21, 23, 29, 30, 32, 34, 36, 37, 41, 42, 44, 47, 51, 55, 63.

Common yew *Taxus baccata*

The elastic qualities of the close-grained wood of the yew were highly prized in the Middle Ages for making longbows such as those with which the English won the Battle of Agincourt. So greatly in demand were yews for bow-making that suitable trees were soon exhausted, and timber had to be imported. The yews that remain, therefore, represent the poorer trees and their descendants. Yew wood, when obtainable, is orange-brown in colour with an attractive grain, and takes a high polish.

Legends abound to explain the presence of yews in churchyards. In most European mythologies the yew was sacred, so the trees may already have been planted at places of pagan worship before the early Christians built their churches on the same sites. Yews were also said to have afforded shelter to early Christian missionaries before their churches were built.

Yews grow especially well on chalk. They resist pollution well and can flourish in the shade of taller trees, but little will grow in the shade they themselves cast. The bark is poisonous and so is the cut or dropped foliage, though horses and cattle sometimes graze on living yew boughs without ill effect. The scarlet berries are harmless, but their seeds are poisonous.

Location

Date

Habitat

Sketches

The tree forms a regular conical shape, with the higher branches ascending and lower branches either level or drooping. It can reach 130 ft (40 m).

All children know this spruce as the familiar Christmas tree.

The light green needles are short and prickly, protruding on all sides of the shoot. The cones are long and cigar-shaped with rounded scales, and they hang down.

SITES GUIDE

A native of continental Europe, the Norway Spruce is widely grown for its timber, or is cut young for sale as Christmas trees.

It may be seen at sites numbers: 1, 4, 8, 10, 12, 26, 34, 37, 38, 42-44, 47, 48, 50, 51.

Male flowers

Female flowers

Flowers open in May. Yellow male flowers cluster at the ends of shoots; erect female flowers are pink; cones ripen in autumn.

Norway spruce *Picea abies*

The Christmas tree so familiar to many a British household is Norway spruce. It is not considered a native tree, but it grew here in pre-glacial times. Driven south by the Ice Age, it was long prevented from re-colonising northern Europe by the east-west barrier of mountain ranges. By the time it had penetrated this barrier, Britain was cut off from the Continent by sea. Although reintroduced by about 1500, its use at Christmas dates only from Victorian times, when Prince Albert brought a Norway spruce to Windsor Castle from Coburg.

The tree serves as much more than a Christmas decoration. It produces a high yield of good-quality timber for building work, pit-props, packing cases and boxes. It is also very suitable for paper pulp, as the wood is composed of long fibres that bind together well.

The timber of Norway spruce is sometimes known as 'violin wood' because of its use for the sounding board, or front, of the violin, and the sound post between front and back. Its function is to transmit vibrations from the strings to the hard maple wood of the sides and back. Pitch and turpentine used to be made from the resin, and a spruce beer from the twigs.

Location	Sketches
Date	
Habitat	

Needles are long, thin and sharp, dark green above and blue-green below. Twigs are yellowish.

Attacks by spruce aphid often defoliate the tree in summer, but seldom kill it.

Female flowers

Male flowers

Male flowers are pale yellow; female flowers, often clustered at the top of the tree, are greenish-red.

Cones are light brown, with crinkled, papery scales and blunt tips.

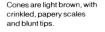

The seeds have thin, papery wings which aid dispersal by wind. [× 5]

This tall, vigorous tree is conical in shape with long, heavy lower branches. It commonly reaches a height of 150 ft (46 m).

Sitka spruce *Picea sitchensis*

Since it was introduced to Britain in 1831, Sitka spruce has become the most widely planted commercial forest tree in the country. It grows quickly on many different types of soil, and yields large quantities of excellent timber. So far it has proved resistant to disease, though in exceptionally dry conditions it may lose its needles to the attacks of the spruce aphid. Deer and voles, which attack other conifers, cause little damage to the Sitka spruce, deterred perhaps by its sharp foliage.

Sitka spruce requires plenty of moisture, and thrives in the wetter areas of western Britain, where conditions resemble those of its native home on the west coast of America. The name Sitka comes from Sitka Sound in Alaska. Because the roots are shallow, trees growing in exposed situations may be uprooted by high winds. The tree is also vulnerable to damage by spring frosts, and in frost hollows the hardier Norway spruce is usually planted.

The white or pale brown wood is light but strong – qualities which made it a suitable material for the construction of Mosquito aircraft during the Second World War. It has long fibres, ideal for paper–making, and it is also used to make boxes.

Location		Sketches
Date		
Habitat		

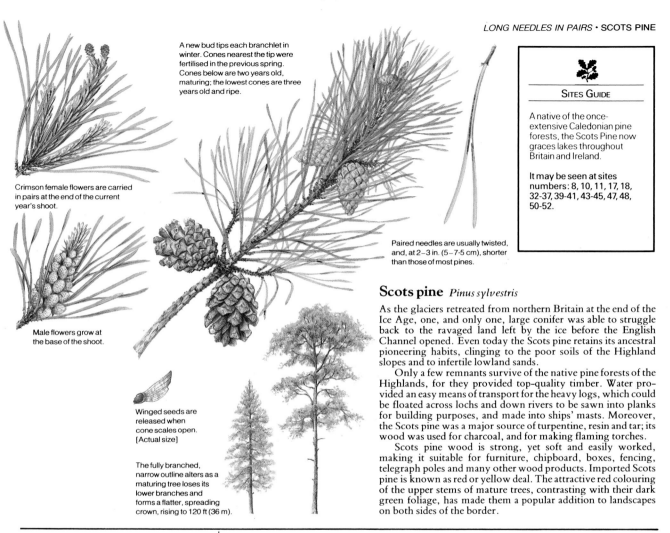

A new bud tips each branchlet in winter. Cones nearest the tip were fertilised in the previous spring. Cones below are two years old, maturing; the lowest cones are three years old and ripe.

Crimson female flowers are carried in pairs at the end of the current year's shoot.

Male flowers grow at the base of the shoot.

Winged seeds are released when cone scales open. [Actual size]

The fully branched, narrow outline alters as a maturing tree loses its lower branches and forms a flatter, spreading crown, rising to 120 ft (36 m).

Paired needles are usually twisted, and, at 2–3 in. (5–7·5 cm), shorter than those of most pines.

Sites Guide

A native of the once-extensive Caledonian pine forests, the Scots Pine now graces lakes throughout Britain and Ireland.

It may be seen at sites numbers: 8, 10, 11, 17, 18, 32-37, 39-41, 43-45, 47, 48, 50-52.

Scots pine *Pinus sylvestris*

As the glaciers retreated from northern Britain at the end of the Ice Age, one, and only one, large conifer was able to struggle back to the ravaged land left by the ice before the English Channel opened. Even today the Scots pine retains its ancestral pioneering habits, clinging to the poor soils of the Highland slopes and to infertile lowland sands.

Only a few remnants survive of the native pine forests of the Highlands, for they provided top-quality timber. Water provided an easy means of transport for the heavy logs, which could be floated across lochs and down rivers to be sawn into planks for building purposes, and made into ships' masts. Moreover, the Scots pine was a major source of turpentine, resin and tar; its wood was used for charcoal, and for making flaming torches.

Scots pine wood is strong, yet soft and easily worked, making it suitable for furniture, chipboard, boxes, fencing, telegraph poles and many other wood products. Imported Scots pine is known as red or yellow deal. The attractive red colouring of the upper stems of mature trees, contrasting with their dark green foliage, has made them a popular addition to landscapes on both sides of the border.

Location

Date

Habitat

Sketches

85

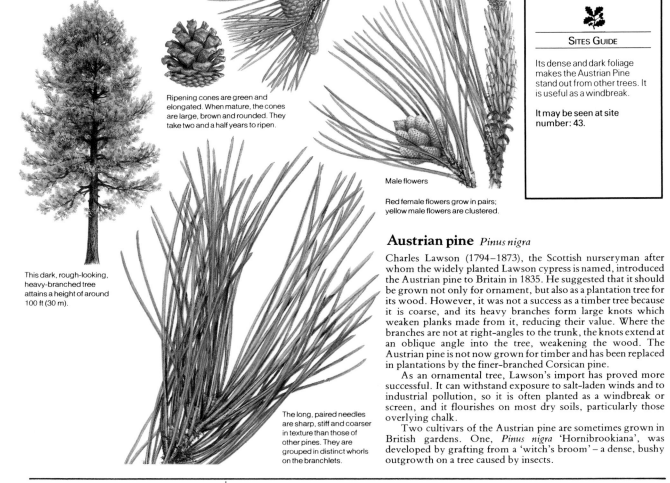

Female flowers

Ripening cones are green and elongated. When mature, the cones are large, brown and rounded. They take two and a half years to ripen.

Male flowers

Red female flowers grow in pairs; yellow male flowers are clustered.

This dark, rough-looking, heavy-branched tree attains a height of around 100 ft (30 m).

The long, paired needles are sharp, stiff and coarser in texture than those of other pines. They are grouped in distinct whorls on the branchlets.

SITES GUIDE

Its dense and dark foliage makes the Austrian Pine stand out from other trees. It is useful as a windbreak.

It may be seen at site number: 43.

Austrian pine *Pinus nigra*

Charles Lawson (1794–1873), the Scottish nurseryman after whom the widely planted Lawson cypress is named, introduced the Austrian pine to Britain in 1835. He suggested that it should be grown not only for ornament, but also as a plantation tree for its wood. However, it was not a success as a timber tree because it is coarse, and its heavy branches form large knots which weaken planks made from it, reducing their value. Where the branches are not at right-angles to the trunk, the knots extend at an oblique angle into the tree, weakening the wood. The Austrian pine is not now grown for timber and has been replaced in plantations by the finer-branched Corsican pine.

As an ornamental tree, Lawson's import has proved more successful. It can withstand exposure to salt-laden winds and to industrial pollution, so it is often planted as a windbreak or screen, and it flourishes on most dry soils, particularly those overlying chalk.

Two cultivars of the Austrian pine are sometimes grown in British gardens. One, *Pinus nigra* 'Hornibrookiana', was developed by grafting from a 'witch's broom' – a dense, bushy outgrowth on a tree caused by insects.

Location

Date

Habitat

Sketches

Female flowers

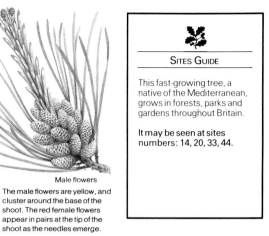

This fast-growing tree, a native of the Mediterranean, grows in forests, parks and gardens throughout Britain.

It may be seen at sites numbers: 14, 20, 33, 44.

Male flowers

The male flowers are yellow, and cluster around the base of the shoot. The red female flowers appear in pairs at the tip of the shoot as the needles emerge.

Corsican pine *Pinus nigra* var. *maritima*

This tree is a variety of Austrian pine, and has much greater value as a timber tree because of its thinner branches and straight, cylindrical trunk. It was introduced to Britain from Corsica in 1799, and proved suitable for planting in the drier areas of the country. Commercial forests of this pine now grow well on the light, sandy soils of the East Anglian Breckland, where they also provide a suitable habitat for deer and birds.

Corsican pine is successful too, on sand dunes, such as those at Culbin, to the east of Inverness, provided that the sand is prevented from moving by 'thatching' it with cut branches. Pines, unlike spruces, grow a thick tap root and few side-shoots, and so hold firm against the wind once the seedlings are established. Corsican pines need plenty of light, and plantations are kept carefully thinned out to encourage the remaining trees to grow quickly.

The timber of the Corsican pine is made into pit props and used in general building work. Some goes into plywood: for this purpose, thin strips of wood are shaved from the log in a spiral, then glued together in layers, the grain running at opposite angles in successive layers for strength.

Needles are long, arranged in pairs on the twig, and sometimes twisted. The mature cone is rounded, and takes two years to ripen. The bud is large and fat, with turned-back scales.

The Corsican pine is a conical tree, slender in outline when young. Its branches are more horizontal than those of other pines. It grows to about 115 ft (35 m).

Location	Sketches
Date	
Habitat	

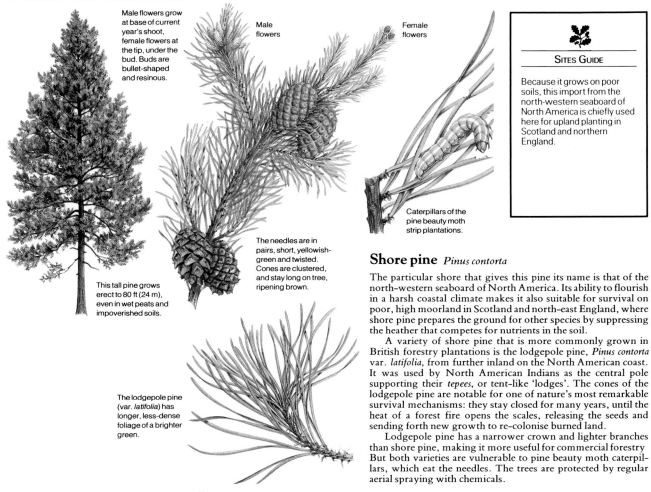

Male flowers grow at base of current year's shoot, female flowers at the tip, under the bud. Buds are bullet-shaped and resinous.

Male flowers

Female flowers

This tall pine grows erect to 80 ft (24 m), even in wet peats and impoverished soils.

The needles are in pairs, short, yellowish-green and twisted. Cones are clustered, and stay long on tree, ripening brown.

Caterpillars of the pine beauty moth strip plantations.

The lodgepole pine (var. *latifolia*) has longer, less-dense foliage of a brighter green.

Shore pine *Pinus contorta*

The particular shore that gives this pine its name is that of the north-western seaboard of North America. Its ability to flourish in a harsh coastal climate makes it also suitable for survival on poor, high moorland in Scotland and north-east England, where shore pine prepares the ground for other species by suppressing the heather that competes for nutrients in the soil.

A variety of shore pine that is more commonly grown in British forestry plantations is the lodgepole pine, *Pinus contorta* var. *latifolia*, from further inland on the North American coast. It was used by North American Indians as the central pole supporting their *tepees*, or tent-like 'lodges'. The cones of the lodgepole pine are notable for one of nature's most remarkable survival mechanisms: they stay closed for many years, until the heat of a forest fire opens the scales, releasing the seeds and sending forth new growth to re-colonise burned land.

Lodgepole pine has a narrower crown and lighter branches than shore pine, making it more useful for commercial forestry But both varieties are vulnerable to pine beauty moth caterpillars, which eat the needles. The trees are protected by regular aerial spraying with chemicals.

Location

Date

Habitat

Sketches

Long, slender needles are a characteristic grass-green. Male flowers crowded at the base of new shoots are yellow in spring. Female flowers are set in clusters of three to five.

Male flowers

Female flowers

The squat, lop-sided cones of the Monterey pine may remain on the tree for many years before falling.

Mature trees have a dense, high dome with many branches; younger trees have a more conical shape. The tree grows to 100 ft (30 m).

Needles are straight and set closely together in groups of three.

On the coast of California, the Monterey pine is low-growing. It grows taller and straighter in Britain. In New Zealand, it has reached 185 ft (56 m).

Monterey pine *Pinus radiata*

The cold that spread out from the Arctic in the Ice Age pushed the conifers of North America southwards. With the retreat of the ice, the trees moved north again, but a small group remained restricted to the Monterey peninsula of California. There – and nowhere else in America – they still survive precariously. The Monterey pine has, however, been successfully introduced to other countries, including Britain, to which it was brought in 1833 by the tree collector David Douglas.

In Britain the tree grows very quickly, and in the south-west continues to grow throughout most of the year. Some trees put on two whorls of branches in a year instead of the single whorl which normally represents a season's growth. The Monterey pine's rapid growth, dense needles and ability to withstand exposure at low altitudes, especially near the sea, make it ideal for planting in rows to form a windbreak. East winds cause excessive water loss and browning of the needles.

Another name for the tree is 'remarkable cone pine'; a reference to its habit of retaining its cones on the tree for 20–30 years. The wood is light, soft, and rather brittle, with light brown heartwood and yellowish sapwood.

Location

Date

Habitat

Sketches

89

In older trees, a long, bare pole ascends to the widely spaced branches of an open crown up to 110 ft (33 m) high.

The stout, grey-green needles are grouped in twos, and longer than those of any other two-needled pine. The long, stalkless cones are clustered and persist for many years on the branches.

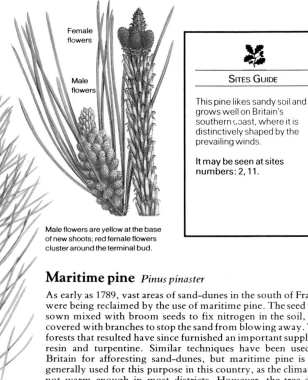

Female flowers

Male flowers

Male flowers are yellow at the base of new shoots; red female flowers cluster around the terminal bud.

Maritime pine *Pinus pinaster*

As early as 1789, vast areas of sand-dunes in the south of France were being reclaimed by the use of maritime pine. The seed was sown mixed with broom seeds to fix nitrogen in the soil, and covered with branches to stop the sand from blowing away. The forests that resulted have since furnished an important supply of resin and turpentine. Similar techniques have been used in Britain for afforesting sand-dunes, but maritime pine is not generally used for this purpose in this country, as the climate is not warm enough in most districts. However, the tree does grow well in the south of England, where it is sometimes known as Bournemouth pine.

Maritime pines grow quickly, and in young plantations the crowns of the trees soon form a wind-resistant barrier. In exposed situations, especially near the sea, the prevailing wind bends the tree at the base of its trunk, compressing the wood on one side; branches are bent over in the same way.

Prehistoric man used such 'compression wood' from pines to make skis; a prehistoric rock-carving in Norway shows that the art of skiing is at least 4,000 years old. Maritime pine has a reddish-brown heartwood and white or yellow sapwood.

Location

Date

Habitat

Sketches

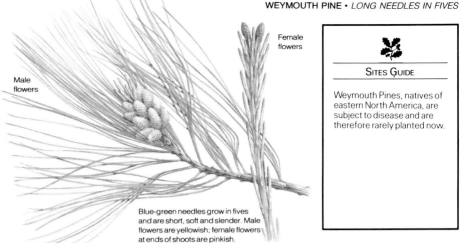

Long cone scales are thickened at the end, like a duck's bill, and open to release seed. [Actual size]

Seed [Actual size]

Male flowers

Female flowers

Blue-green needles grow in fives and are short, soft and slender. Male flowers are yellowish; female flowers at ends of shoots are pinkish.

Pointed, banana-shaped cones are 4–6 in. (10–15 cm) long, on short stalks. They often bear white resin.

Mature trees have an irregular conical shape, with upswept or horizontal branches. Shoots on the upper branches are spiky. Trees grow to 115 ft (35 m).

Blister-rust is caused by a fungus which passes through most of its life-cycle on the leaves of blackcurrants.

Weymouth pine *Pinus strobus*

The Duchess of Beaufort introduced this North American pine to England in 1705. It grew well on her estate at Badminton, Gloucestershire; however, the tree was not named after her. That honour went to Lord Weymouth who, a short while later, planted the pine extensively on his domains at Longleat, Wiltshire. It was valued for its excellent timber, which was used for building and for making boxes.

Unfortunately, the tree is subject to a fungal disease called blister-rust, which attacks the upper stem. Ultimately this kills the pine, so it is no longer planted on a commercial scale. The disease crossed from Europe to America in 1892, where it spread rapidly and caused extensive damage. The fungus lives for part of its life on fruit bushes such as blackcurrants, and the Weymouth pine is at risk wherever these bushes grow. Trees whose bark has been damaged by the rust are often attacked by voles, which find the damaged bark palatable.

The pine grows rapidly and is resistant to frost. It thrives on light, moist soils and can live to between 100 and 200 years old. Today, most Weymouth pines in Britain are old trees in parks and churchyards, as few young ones have been planted.

Location	Sketches
Date	
Habitat	

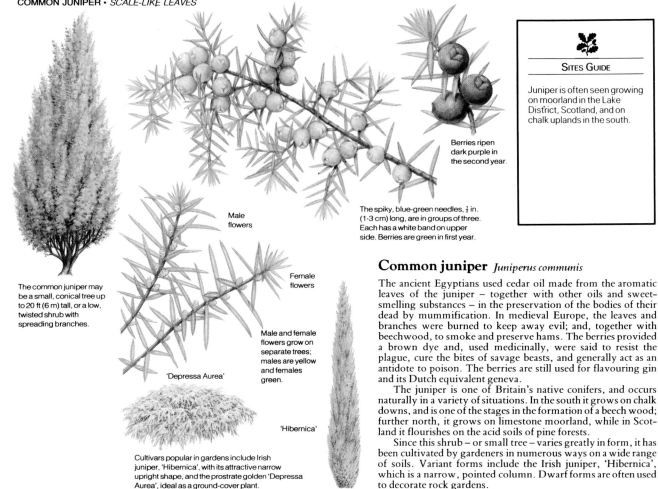

Berries ripen
dark purple in
the second year.

The spiky, blue-green needles, ½ in.
(1·3 cm) long, are in groups of three.
Each has a white band on upper
side. Berries are green in first year.

Male
flowers

Female
flowers

Male and female
flowers grow on
separate trees;
males are yellow
and females
green.

'Depressa Aurea'

'Hibernica'

The common juniper may
be a small, conical tree up
to 20 ft (6 m) tall, or a low,
twisted shrub with
spreading branches.

Cultivars popular in gardens include Irish
juniper, 'Hibernica', with its attractive narrow
upright shape, and the prostrate golden 'Depressa
Aurea', ideal as a ground-cover plant.

Common juniper *Juniperus communis*

The ancient Egyptians used cedar oil made from the aromatic
leaves of the juniper – together with other oils and sweet-
smelling substances – in the preservation of the bodies of their
dead by mummification. In medieval Europe, the leaves and
branches were burned to keep away evil; and, together with
beechwood, to smoke and preserve hams. The berries provided
a brown dye and, used medicinally, were said to resist the
plague, cure the bites of savage beasts, and generally act as an
antidote to poison. The berries are still used for flavouring gin
and its Dutch equivalent geneva.

The juniper is one of Britain's native conifers, and occurs
naturally in a variety of situations. In the south it grows on chalk
downs, and is one of the stages in the formation of a beech wood;
further north, it grows on limestone moorland, while in Scotland it flourishes on the acid soils of pine forests.

Since this shrub – or small tree – varies greatly in form, it has
been cultivated by gardeners in numerous ways on a wide range
of soils. Variant forms include the Irish juniper, 'Hibernica',
which is a narrow, pointed column. Dwarf forms are often used
to decorate rock gardens.

Location		Sketches
Date		
Habitat		

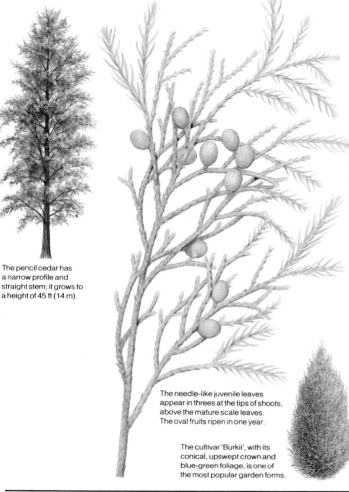

The pencil cedar has a narrow profile and straight stem; it grows to a height of 45 ft (14 m).

The needle-like juvenile leaves appear in threes at the tips of shoots, above the mature scale leaves. The oval fruits ripen in one year.

The cultivar 'Burkii', with its conical, upswept crown and blue-green foliage, is one of the most popular garden forms.

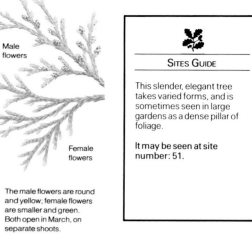

Male flowers

Female flowers

The male flowers are round and yellow; female flowers are smaller and green. Both open in March, on separate shoots.

SITES GUIDE

This slender, elegant tree takes varied forms, and is sometimes seen in large gardens as a dense pillar of foliage.

It may be seen at site number: 51.

Pencil cedar *Juniperus virginiana*

As its name suggests, the wood of this cedar used to be much in demand for making pencils, as it is easily sharpened and does not splinter. Today, however, the tree is no longer so abundant, and its wood is used only in the manufacture of the finest quality pencils. The wood is light, soft and aromatic, and has a fine texture, with rose-red heartwood and white sapwood. It is durable and resists attacks by insects, and has been used to make moth-proof linings for chests and wardrobes; wood shavings from the tree used to be put in drawers to keep moths away. Cedar oil is an ingredient of some soaps and perfumes.

The pencil cedar, tallest of the junipers, was introduced from eastern North America to England as an ornamental tree in 1664. It is hardy and very adaptable, growing in a wide variety of situations; it does particularly well on drier soils. Like the common juniper, it is very slow-growing, and appears in dwarf form in rockeries.

The aromatic leaves are needle-like when young. Older trees develop cypress-like leaves, but juvenile leaves are often retained at the branch tips; some cultivated varieties never develop adult foliage.

Location	Sketches
Date	
Habitat	

The small, densely packed, leaves are bright green and very like those of Lawson cypress. The inconspicuous green female flowers and yellow male flowers appear infrequently.

Female flowers

Male flowers

Sites Guide

This hardy, fast-growing natural hybrid is found on a variety of soils and sites, and is very popular for hedges.

The Leyland cypress has a narrow, column-like crown. Its numerous branches extend from crown to base. It has reached a height of 100 ft (30 m) in Britain.

[×2]

The round, brown cones occur only occasionally, at the tips of branches. Small winged seeds have so far been only rarely produced.

Leyland cypress × *Cupressocyparis leylandii*

Although hybrids occur quite frequently between closely related trees, it is not often that a cross occurs naturally between trees of different genera. This happened when the cones of Nootka cypress (a 'false' cypress of the *Chamaecyparis* genus), were fertilised by pollen from Monterey cypress (a true cypress of the *Cupressus* genus). The cross took place in 1888 on the Leighton Estate, Welshpool, and the hybrid was given the name of C. J. Leyland, brother-in-law of the owner of the estate, who took some of the seedlings and planted them on his own estate at Haggerston Castle in Northumberland.

Twenty-three years later, a further cross occurred at Leighton Estate. This time the cones of the Monterey cypress were fertilised by pollen from the Nootka cypress. The result of this cross was a second hybrid, given the name of 'Leighton Green'.

The first cross is known as 'Haggerston Grey', as its scale-like leaves are often grey at the base. It is now the most commonly grown of the two crosses. In either form, Leyland cypress combines the hardiness of Nootka cypress with the fast growth of Monterey cypress; in fact, it is the fastest-growing conifer in Britain, growing as much as 4 ft (1·25 m) a year.

Location

Date

Habitat

Sketches

The single upright leading shoot at the top of this tree distinguishes it from the cypresses that it otherwise resembles. It grows rapidly in damp, cool areas, reaching a height of about 83 ft (25 m) in 30 years.

The leaves are broader than those of cypresses, bright green on top with white patches below. The leafy cones mature in one year.

Female flowers

Male flowers

Male and female flowers are borne at the end of short branches. The male flowers are reddish, the female flowers yellowish-green, opening in March.

Western red cedar *Thuja plicata*

North American Indians used the timber of western red cedar for their canoes and totem poles. Today it is familiar in Britain as the reddish-brown wood used for the roofing shingles and wall cladding of modern bungalows, and for garden sheds. The American Indians discovered many centuries ago that the fibrous timber cleaves readily; the fibres are therefore not cut, so that water runs off easily and the wood does not decay.

The tree was introduced to Britain in 1853, when it was sent from the west coast of North America to the nurseries of John Veitch in Exeter. It quickly became popular as an ornamental tree, being particularly suitable for formal avenues and hedges, and in 1876 it was first planted as a forest tree at Benmore in Argyllshire. It is planted under other trees because it does not mind shade, and its narrow shape makes it ideal as a 'nurse' crop to shelter young oaks, because its branches do not spread and damage the surrounding trees.

In its native land the western red cedar grows from Alaska to California. It is not a true cedar, but was given its name by early settlers who believed it to be related to the cedars of Lebanon mentioned in the Bible.

Location

Date

Habitat

Sketches

95

Inverness

50 · · 48 Aberdeen
51

49 · · 48

· 47

· 46

Glasgow   Edinburgh

44

45

43 ·

63 · · 64

42 ·

41 · Newcastle-upon-Tyne

Lough
Neagh

52 · Belfast

40
39 · · 37
38 · · 36

· 62

Aire   Leeds

61 ·
60 ·

Kingston upon Hull

Shannon

Dublin

Liverpool   Manchester

Bangor

31

32

58 ·
57 ·

Suir

59 ·

30

35

34 ·

Norwich

28 ·
29

Severn

Birmingham

Gt Ouse

Blackwater

27 ·

56 · · 54
· 55
· 53

Cork

24 ·

26

33 ·

Thames

23 ·   22

Cardiff

25 ·   21
London

Bristol

14 ·

9
8 · · 10

Parret

12 ·

19
17 · · 20
18

13 ·   15 ·

16 ·

7 ·

6 · Exeter

Southampton

11 ·

4 · · 5

2 ·   · 3

Truro

1 ·

0   50
MILES

96

The Sites

A descriptive gazetteer of places around Britain to see the woodland trees on pages 12-95.

Order

The sites are featured in a special order, designed for ease of reference. They follow each other in an order determined by th Ordnance Survey's grid reference system, which works from west to east, and from south to north. The first sites described are those in Cornwall, in other words those furthest west and furthest south; the last sites described on mainland Britain are in north-east Scotland; Ulster and the Republic of Ireland are listed separately at the end.

For additional ease of reference, the sites are however grouped in regions and counties, and this framework takes precedence over the order required by the grid system; so that for example, all the sites in Wales, from south to north, are listed together; then the list continues, starting afresh with the south-west corner of the Midlands, ie Gloucestershire.

Location of sites

Each site is described in terms of access from a nearby major road or town, or other major landmark. The number of the Ordnance Survey Landranger Sheet (scale 1:50 000) on which the site occurs is also given, together with a grid reference number for exact and speedy location of the site on the map. (Full directions on how to read a numerical grid reference are given on all Landranger Sheets.) A six-figure grid reference number is accurate to the nearest hundred metres and these are given where possible; however, it is sometimes more appropriate to quote a four-figure grid reference, accurate to the nearest kilometre, when a large area is in question.

Tree names in bold type

Tree names in bold are those which are featured in the identification section, pages 12-95.

Botanical terms

A glossary explaining all botanical terms in the text is given on page 124.

KEY TO MAP
1 Lanhydrock
2 Trelissick
3 Tremayne Woods
4 Hembury Woods
5 Castle Drogo
6 Teign Valley Woods
7 Killerton
8 Arlington Court
9 Watersmeet
10 Holnicote
11 Brownsea Island
12 Stourhead
13 Mottisfont Abbey
14 Woolton Hill
15 Selborne Common
16 Slindon
17 Witley Common
18 Leith Hill
19 Ranmore Common
20 Box Hill
21 Cliveden

22 Bishopston Valley
23 Stackpole
24 Dolaucothi
25 Bradenham Woods
26 Brockhampton
27 Croft Castle
28 Attingham Park
29 Dudmaston
30 Dovedale
31 Styal
32 Clumber Park
33 Ashridge Estate
34 Blickling Hall
35 Felbrigg Hall
36 Brigsteer Woods
37 Claife Woods
38 Nether Wasdale
39 Manesty Park
40 Great Wood, Derwentwater
41 Allen Banks
42 Wallington
43 Cragside

44 Brodick Castle
45 Culzean
46 Dollar Glen
47 The Hermitage
48 Linn of Tummel
49 Pass of Killiecrankie
50 Crathes
51 Drum Castle
52 The Argory
53 Glengarriff
54 Derrycunnihy/Ladies View
55 Muckross Wood/Old Kenmare Road
56 Caragh Lake
57 Glenstal
58 Cahermurphy
59 Avondale Forest Park
60 Lough Inagh
61 Old Head
62 Union Wood
63 Glenveagh National Park
64 Rathmullan Wood/Hollymount

THE SOUTH WEST

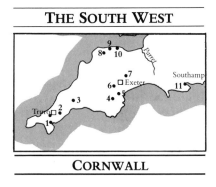

CORNWALL

1 Lanhydrock

LOCATION **Two-and-a-half miles (4 km) south of Bodmin on the road to Lostwithiel (B3268);** *Landranger Sheet 200, SX085636;* OPEN **Apr to end-Oct: every day including Good Fri and bank holidays 11-6. Nov to end Mar: garden only open every day during daylight hours;** ADMISSION **(garden and grounds only) £1.50, children £0.75.**

Lanhydrock overlooks the valley of the River Fowey. The garden is set on a hillside facing north-east above the house and park and is flanked by woodland, which acts as a shelterbelt. The main part of the 'higher Garden' contrasts with the formal area near the house and affords views on to the park with its prominent double avenue.

Highlights
Beech and to a lesser extent **lime, sycamore, oak** and **yew** are important to the character of Lanhydrock as is the scattering of conifers, including **Monterey Pine.** It is also the only

National Trust garden in Cornwall to boast five species of **birch. Small-leaved Lime** is a recent introduction. Six varieties of **rowan** can be seen, which display a range of berry colour – white, pinkish, yellow and red.

Some of the old **sycamore** that were planted in the 18th C remain in the double avenue, but during the 19th C and 20th C, they were interplanted with **beech.** Beyond the double avenue is Station Drive, where mature specimens of **Sitka Spruce, Norway Spruce, Douglas Fir, Western Red Cedar** and **Western Hemlock** can be seen.

2 Trelissick

LOCATION **Four miles (6.5 km) south of Truro, on both sides of the B3289 above King Harry Ferry;** *Landranger Sheet 204, SW837396;* OPEN **(garden only) Mar to end-Oct: Mon to Sat including Good Friday 11-6, Sun 1-6 or sunset if earlier. Woodland walk also open Nov to end-Mar;** ADMISSION **£1.50, children £0.75.**

Trelissick is situated on land sloping eastward towards the estuary of the River Fal. The garden is on each side of a valley, bisected by the B3289. To the north of the road, crossed by bridge, is a young arboretum called the Carcadden, while the part to the south comprises a woodland garden, lawns and shrub borders.

Highlights
The earliest trees planted in the park and garden date from mid- to late-18th C.

By 1842, the main garden area consisted of mixed woodland of **Common Beech, English Oak,** Holm Oak and **Sweet Chestnut.** One of Trelissick's owners, C.D. Gilbert, planted conifers, such as **Maritime** and **Monterey Pine,** on a large scale at the end of the 19th C.

In the Carcadden, conifers are also conspicuous, some of the most remarkable being the two Monterey Cypresses planted there in 1948. They can best be appreciated across the entrance path. **Sycamore** and **Norway Maple** are prominent in the Carcadden; an astonishing 28 varieties of *Acer* can be found at Trelissick.

Sadly, many **elms** in the parkland were recently lost to disease, and only a few survive. The remainder have been replaced by new plantings of **oak, beech** and other broad-leaves.

3 Tremayne Woods

LOCATION **South-east of Helston; access on foot at Mudgeon on the Manaccan road, 1½ miles (2.5 km) east of Mawgan;** *Landranger Sheet 204, SW728257;* OPEN **at all times;** ADMISSION **free.**

Tremayne Woods are a fine example of western, or 'oceanic', coppice oakwoods, which have developed a varied and distinctive flora, rich in mosses and lichens thriving in the damp conditions beneath the tree canopy. Coppicing probably ended about the turn of the century, and the trees have grown tall on this sheltered site on the south bank of the Helford River and its tidal creeks.

Highlights

A network of paths leads through the woods from where there are beautiful views across the water. **Oak, beech, sycamore, ash** and **elm** are all present, with **alder** in the wetter places along the valley bottom. The **beech** were planted about the mid-19th C and are now reaching maturity.

DEVON

---

4 Hembury Woods

LOCATION **Two miles (3 km) north of Buckfastleigh, north of the A384;** *Landranger Sheet 202, SX726684;* OPEN at all times; ADMISSION free.

The main area of Hembury is a Site of Special Scientific Interest (SSSI) and consists of **oak**-dominated woodland, partly underplanted with **beech** and conifers. It is typical of the former coppice oakwood in the steep-sided valleys surrounding Dartmoor, and it contains a fine variety of woodland structure.

Highlights

From the car park, which is situated south of the road, cross the road and follow the paths towards the River Dart. Then walk north along the west side of the river bank, through mature woodland, dominated by **beech.** There are scattered mature **Norway Spruce** planted as ornamental trees in the early years of this century. Inland, there are stands of **oak** coppice. On the shallower soils, the poorer quality **oak** was underplanted with **beech, Western Hemlock** and **Western Red Cedar** in the 1950s and 1960s.

Along the tributary stream valley, towards Hembury Barn, older 'maiden' **oak** are found with **alder** along the stream itself.

---

5 Castle Drogo

LOCATION **At Drewsteignton, 4 miles (6.5 km) south of the Exeter to Okehampton road via Crockernwell;** *Landranger Sheet 191, SX-721900;* OPEN **Apr to end-Oct: every day 11-6;** ADMISSION **(garden and grounds only) £1.20.**

Perhaps the principal feature here is extensive areas of relatively undisturbed old **oak** coppice. The two main areas, Whiddon and Drewston Woods, are typical of such woodlands in southern Devon. The whole estate makes delightful walking, but keep to public rights of way.

Highlights

South-east of the castle is Whiddon Wood, on the far side of the spectacular gorge of the River Teign. On the north bank, heather and bracken on the steep upper slope merge into **birch** and **oak.** The **oaks,** which have now grown to about 30 ft (10 m), were coppiced in the past. Beside the river itself, large, older **oak** are mixed with **ash, beech** and **sycamore.**

In Drewston Wood, the **oaks** are a uniform 40 ft (12 m) in height, mainly English, and one-/two-/three-stemmed.

This wood lies to the north-east of the property, and has its southern border along the north bank of the River Teign, where visitors will find appreciable numbers of **alder.**

---

6 Teign Valley Woods

LOCATION **Three miles (5 km) north-east of Moretonhampstead, on both sides of the B3212;** *Landranger Sheet 191, SX795885;* OPEN at all times; ADMISSION free.

Here are many acres of spectacular hanging woodland, mainly **oak** coppice, situated along the River Teign near Steps Bridge. They are an excellent example of the type of habitat produced by coppicing, a management system that must have been continued here well into the 20th C. The property makes an important contribution to the wooded valley system of the Teign Valley, itself of importance as part of the delightful wooded fringes of Dartmoor, which contrast with the wilderness of the interior.

Highlights

The **oak** coppice consists of single and two- to three-stemmed trees forming a fairly low canopy 15-30 ft (5-10 m) in height. In the stream valleys, at the base of slopes and at the edges of the woodland, the structure is more diverse and a greater range of trees are present. These include **alder, sycamore** and **beech,** mostly of coppice origin; also **Wych Elm** and one specimen of **Wild Service Tree** in St Thomas Cleave Wood – the main wood on the west side of the B3212.

7 Killerton

LOCATION Seven miles (11 km) north-east of Exeter on the west side of the road to Cullompton (B3181, formerly A38); the entrance is off the B3185; *Landranger Sheet 192, SX989970;* OPEN during daylight hours throughout the year; ADMISSION (garden and park only) £1.50, children £0.75.

Killerton has a fine arboretum through which delightful walks can be made. It is laid out on the slopes of Killerton Clump, a basalt 'plug' rising steeply from the surrounding farmland on Old Red Sandstone. In 1808 the Acland family employed the famous nurseryman John Veitch to plant the original trees of the Beech Avenue, and, once his firm had moved to Exeter in 1832, Killerton regularly received trees from his nursery.

Highlights
A memorably interesting day can be spent at Killerton walking amongst **beech, birch, lime** and numerous species of conifer. The spectacular views and colourful foliage around the garden will greatly add to your enjoyment. At the east end of the Beech Avenue are **Sweet Chestnuts** planted by John Veitch at the same time as the original **beeches.**

8 Arlington Court

LOCATION Seven miles (11 km) north-east of Barnstaple, on the east side of the A39; *Landranger Sheet 180, SS611405;* OPEN (garden and park only) Apr to end-Oct: every day 11-6. Nov to end-Mar: during daylight hours; ADMISSION (garden, grounds and stable only) £1.50, children £0.75.

The woods at Arlington Court are a fine example of an inland wooded valley system adjacent to Exmoor. The upper slopes, up to 600 ft (200 m) above sea level, are exposed to the strong westerly gales, but in the sheltered valley bottoms some particularly fine specimens occur.

Highlights
A feature of the old **oak** and **beech** at Arlington is the profusion of mosses, lichens and ferns growing on their trunks and branches. These thrive in the wet climate of North Devon. Above the pond beside the church (in front of the house) a small collection of unusual **ash** varieties was planted in 1970 – well worth stopping to appreciate.

The main wooded areas are a mosaic of mature mixed woodland and young plantations dating from the 1950s. A circular walk leads through Lodge Plantation and Brockham Plantation to Arlington Lake, and returns through the Wilderness on the east side of the garden. Originally these areas were mainly **oak, beech** and **Sweet Chestnut,** but, when the garden was extended in the 19th C, conifers were introduced, chiefly Common Silver Fir and **larch.** The later plantings include **beech, Douglas Fir, Western Hemlock** and **Norway Spruce,** besides young **oak.** The walk is a useful way to these features.

9 Watersmeet

LOCATION East of Lynmouth, on both sides of the A39. Cars should be parked 2 miles (3 km) up the road from Lynmouth to Barnstaple (A39); it is only a short walk down to Watersmeet. From there a network of paths leads up both sides of the River Lyn and along the steep tree-clad slopes; *Landranger Sheet 180, SS7449;* OPEN at all times; ADMISSION free.

Watersmeet is typical of the old coppice oakwoods of North Devon. It is a Site of Special Scientific Interest (SSSI) on account of the extent of the woods, their largely undisturbed semi-natural canopy, the high diversity of stand types and tree species and the clear correlation between stand type and slope angle, soil moisture and so on.

Highlights.
Many different stand types occur. The common pattern of distribution is to find **oak** coppice on steep slopes and well-drained soils, and **oak** with various mixtures of **ash, Wych Elm** and **alder** in the valley bottoms. The **oak** coppice is mixed with **birch** on the most freely draining soil, and with **hazel** where the soil is slightly more moist. **Oak** high forest is also present.

Scattered throughout the wood are specimens of the very rare Devon Whitebeam, *Sorbus devoniensis* and *S. subcuneata.* These are recognized as separate species, but are very hard for the layman to distinguish from the **Common Whitebeam.**

South of the Watersmeet road is Lyn

Cleave, where **sycamore** and **ash** are dominant in uniform-aged trees. **Sweet Chestnut, elm, yew, holly, beech, rowan, Downy Birch** and **oak** are also present. To the east the **ash-sycamore** woodland becomes a **Sessile Oak** coppice with some **elm, ash** and **alder**.

SOMERSET

---

10 Holnicote

LOCATION **East and south of Porlock, astride the A39, extending 6 miles (9.5 km) south from the north coast. Car parks are scattered throughout the property; Landranger Sheet 181, SS8844;** OPEN **at all times;** ADMISSION **free.**

Holnicote Estate is one of the finest wooded properties belonging to the National Trust. It contains extensive hillside and valley woodlands within the eastern half of the Exmoor National Park and these are an essential part of the general Exmoor landscape. In addition to natural woodlands, there are also numerous plantations, mainly of conifer. An example of just how well a correctly sited plantation can fit into the general landscape is provided by the Luccombe area, which supports mixed conifers planted in the 1920s. Much of Holnicote Estate, which extends for 12,000 acres, is a Site of Special Scientific Interest (SSSI).

Highlights
One of the largest continuous blocks of **Sessile Oak** wood in the country is at Horner Woods, which also have a great variety of slopes and aspects. The valley bottoms support large mature **oak** and **ash**, with **alder** and **elm** locally.

Many miles of footpaths lead through the Horner Woods, and through the Lucombe and Selworthy plantations on either side of the Porlock Vale. Many were named by the Acland family, who gave the property to the National Trust in 1949. Sir Francis Acland chaired the committee that set up the Forestry Commission in 1919. The plantations of **Scots Pine, larch** and **Douglas Fir** which he established in the 1920s are now mature and are being replaced with similar mixtures.

In addition to the conifer areas, there are some deciduous plantations of **beech** and **oak** as well as some mixed plantations.

DORSET

---

11 Brownsea Island

LOCATION **This the largest island in Poole Harbour and is reached by boat from Pooole Quay and from Sandbanks; Landranger Sheet 195, SZ025880;** OPEN **Apr to end-Sept: daily 10-8 or dusk if earlier;** ADMISSION **£0.80.**

Brownsea Island has an interesting diversity of woodland, itself an important part of the Island's ecosystem, providing habitats for many species of fauna. The Island is a Site of Special Scientific Interest (SSSI) and a Grade I Nature Conservations Review Site.

Highlights
Most of the woodland is secondary **birch** and **pine**, including **Maritime Pine**, which seeded in naturally after a disastrous fire in 1935. A few of the very large **Scots Pine** of the previous generation can be seen at the eastern end of the Island.

The scrub-woodland of **birch** and **willow** occurs at intervals along the west and part of the south coast and provides some diversity of structure.

An **alder** carr can be found on the edge of the marshy ground forming the boundary of the Nature Reserve managed by the Dorset Naturalists' Trust (guided walks daily during the summer). Large Holm Oak overhang the beach to the west of the Quay, and behind them, near the former kitchen gardens, is an area of mature mixed deciduous woodland, including **oak, beech** and **Sweet Chestnut**.

THE SOUTH EAST

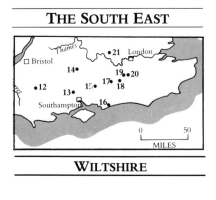

WILTSHIRE

12 Stourhead

LOCATION At the village of Stourton on the B3092, 2 miles (5 km) north-west of Mere (A303); *Landranger Sheet 183, ST7735;* OPEN (garden only) all year: every day 8-7 or sunset if earlier; ADMISSION (garden only) Mar to mid-May, mid-June to end-Nov £1.50, children £0.80. Mid-May to mid-June £2, children £1. Dec to end-Feb £0.80, children £0.40.

Stourhead garden, with its pleasure garden, lakes and temples, is one of Britain's finest examples of 18th C landscape design, and it contains many magnificent old trees. The areas of high ground consist principally of indigenous **beech** and **oak** and act as a frame for the garden. The most continuous area of high ground is the Shades, which is notable for its fine hanging **beech** woods.

Highlights

The principal species at Stourhead are **beech, oak** and **Sweet Chestnut,** many of which were planted by Henry Hoare in the mid 18th C and can still be seen today. **Beech** was the most often planted, and some magnificent specimens can be found in the Shades, the area that runs from near the village entrance north-westwards, parallel with Garden Lake. Heights of up to 125 ft (40 m) have been recorded.

Other woodland trees of interest around the lake include **Western Hemlock, Sitka Spruce** and a 20 ft (6.5 m) 'dwarf' **Norway Spruce.** A very large **Western Red Cedar** in the pinetum, north-west of the pleasure garden, is regarded as one of the earliest plantings in Britain, about 1854. This specimen has formed a cathedral of a tree with the lowest branches layered; the visitor can walk inside its crown. Of a similar age is a **Douglas Fir** by Turner's Paddock Lake.

HAMPSHIRE

13 Mottisfont Abbey

LOCATION Four-and-a-half miles (7 km) north-west of Romsey, ¾ mile west of the A3057; *Landranger Sheet 185, SU327270;* OPEN (grounds only) Apr to end-Sept: Sun to Thurs 2-6; ADMISSION (grounds only) Apr to end-May, Aug to end-Sept £1.00, June to end-July £1.20.

The single greatest attraction to Mottisfont Abbey gardens is a spectacular giant London Plane, growing on the lawns beside the River Test.

It is 100 ft (30 m) high and has the largest girth of any in the country. Tree-lovers are drawn from many miles around to wonder at this marvellous specimen.

Highlights

Wandering around these peaceful grounds, you may well be surprised how many fine woodland trees are flourishing despite the shallow, chalky soil. The garden contains large specimens of **walnut, sycamore, Sweet Chestnut** and **beech,** some of considerable age. Oldest of all is the famous Mottisfont **Oak,** the short, thick trunk of which can be seen from the gate at the end of the river walk. It may be as much as 800 years old; it is certainly as old as the medieval priory.

14 Woolton Hill

LOCATION On the west side of the road to Andover, (A343), 3 miles (5 km) south-west of Newbury; *Landranger Sheet 174, SU442627;* OPEN at all times; ADMISSION free.

Woolton Hill belonged to an amateur forester who planted many conifers amid this essentially broad-leaved woodland. It is a secluded property, gently sloping in an easterly direction, and there is a small artificial lake in the north-east corner.

Highlights

Conifer plantations, many of quite recent origin, characterize almost the entire property, although in the south-west corner a small block of **beech** woodland remains. The conifers, especially **Corsican Pine,** have grown well and some fine specimens abound.

Of the remaining broad-leaves, **English Oak** and **Common Beech** prevail, with **birch, rowan, holly** and **hazel** also scattered throughout Woolton Hill. **Sweet Chestnut** is also found. Around the lake and along the chalk stream is a dense stand of **alder,** which has been recently coppiced in places.

15 Selborne Common

LOCATION West of the B3006, between Selborne and Newton Valence, 4 miles (6.5 km) south of Alton; *Landranger Sheet 186, SU735333;* OPEN at all times; ADMISSION free.

Selborne Common has become famous through the works of Gilbert White, who lived here all his life and who wrote *The Natural History of Selborne.* In these ancient woodlands **beech** predominates amid other natives, and a few conifers. Selborne Common has a steep, north-east facing, chalk escarpment and a plateau behind from which there are marvellous views southwards. Much of the woodland is a Site of Special Scientific Interest (SSSI). Nearby, to the east of the church, are the Short and Long Lythes, which boast some magnificent hanging **beech** woods on the slopes overlooking the Oakhanger stream.

Highlights
The very steep north-east facing slope is

virutally a pure **beech** wood, with occasional **ash, sycamore** and **English Oak.** The **beech** trees are of varying ages. The south- and north-facing slopes are similarly covered, mainly with **beech,** while in the woodland on the chalk plateau broad-leaved natives are evenly mixed. On the western edge of Selborne Common, **English Oak** prevails; two other areas were planted in 1960 and 1961 with **beech** and **larch.**

WEST SUSSEX

16 Slindon

LOCATION Slindon Park Wood is accessible through the Lodge Gates off the A29, just north of Bognor Regis; *Landranger Sheet 197, SU9608;* OPEN daily until dusk; ADMISSION free.

The Slindon Estate encompasses 3,500 acres of farm and woodland astride the South Downs. Although it is only possible to take in this extensive landscape by long-distance footpaths, there is one particular area well worth a special visit: Slindon Park Wood.

Highlights
Slindon Park Wood enfolds the old park extending below Slindon House. Here the ancient park boundary banks are visible and these enclose 48 acres of truly magnificent old **beech,** now over 250 years old and 125 ft (40 m) in height. They are gradually succumbing to old age and windblow, but a dense growth

of young natural seedlings has become established beneath them, to continue their beauty for another generation.

SURREY

17 Witley Common

LOCATION Half a mile (0.8 km) south-west of Milford, between the A3 and the A286; *Landranger Sheet 186, SU9240;* OPEN Apr to end-Oct: every day except Mon and Fri (but open bank holiday Mon) 11-1, 2-5. Nov: Sat and Sun 1.30-4; ADMISSION free.

Witley and the adjoining Milford Common comprise 377 acres of woodland, wet heath and open land with a varied and interesting flora. Set in pine woods on the edge of the Common is the Witley Information Centre, which houses a fascinating audio-visual programme and displays illustrating the history and development of the range of habitats here.

Highlights
The principal trees are **Scots Pine,** which regenerates freely on the Surrey heaths, **English Oak, Silver Birch** and **Sweet Chestnut.** Following the Nature Trails, you may, with a searching eye, also find **Common Beech, hornbeam, ash, English Elm, sycamore, Norway Maple, Field Maple, Wild Service Tree, whitebeam, rowan, holly** and **yew. Larch** and **Douglas Fir** are also present.

18 Leith Hill

LOCATION **Off B2126 on the road to Forest Green, 2 miles (3 km) from Ockley (A29);** *Landranger Sheet 87, TQ1343;* OPEN **at all times;** ADMISSION **free.**

This extensive area contains a wide variety of woodland types, and, together with the remaining areas of heath and numerous small streams, these form a site of considerable diversity – much of which is a Site of Special Scientific Interest (SSSI).

Highlights
The National Trust's property at Leith Hill is divided into several separate pieces, the largest being Leith Hill Place (including Leith Hill Wood). In the Wood occur **oak** and coppiced **hazel,** with **ash, beech** and **hornbeam** in parts, as well as **alder** and **Field Maple** along the stream. On the east side of the road is an **oak** and **birch** woodland with some fine **oaks** 150 to 180 years old and several flushes of **alder. Beech, ash, yew** and **hornbeam** also occur and some **hazel, Sweet Chestnut** and **sycamore** coppice.

Nearby is Leith Hill summit, where **oak, birch** and **Scots Pine** are to be found, and farther east is Mosses Wood, in and around The Landslip, on both sides of another road, mainly comprising **beech** planted with **Scots Pine** and **larch.** Duke's Warren, to the north, has well-structured woodland where **oak, birch** and **Scots Pine** are prevalent with some **beech, rowan** and **holly.** There is also an interesting valley of **alder** and **birch.**

Slightly removed from the main complex of Leith Hill is Severells Copse, near Friday Street. This is probably an ancient woodland site and it has **oak** with **birch** or **hazel. Scots Pine** is frequent, but nowhere dominant; **alder** flourishes along the stream to the west of the copse.

19 Ranmore Common

LOCATION **Two miles (3 km) north-west of Dorking, adjoining the southern boundary of Polesden Lacey estate;** *Landranger Sheet 187, TQ1451;* OPEN **at all times;** ADMISSION **free.**

Ranmore Common is a predominantly semi-natural **beech** woodland of over 700 acres, situated on well-drained chalky soil on the southern slopes of the North Downs. There are various bridle and footpaths along which to explore this beautiful, peaceful area.

Highlights
In this entirely broad-leaved woodland the dominant species, **beech,** occurs widely in both valleys and on spurs. **English Oak, holly** and **birch** also grow throughout the area and are often concentrated on high spots, whereas **ash** is prevalent in patches at the bottom of the slope. **Yew** is widely scattered on spurs and in valleys.

20 Box Hill

LOCATION **One mile (1.5 km) north of Dorking, on the A24;** approach by the steep zig-zag road from Burford Bridge; *Landranger Sheet 187, TQ171511;* OPEN **at all times;** ADMISSION **free.**

Box Hill, on the edge of the North Downs, is both a Country Park and a Site of Special Scientific Interest (SSSI) designated by the Nature Conservancy Council. There is extensive woodland – nearly 1,000 acres – with two distinct soil types: one shallow and alkaline, the other deeper and slightly acid.

Highlights
Footpaths from the main car park and visitor centre at the top of the hill lead through mature **beech** woods in which **Wild Cherry** may be found. There are also young plantations of **beech** mixed with **European Larch** and **Corsican Pine** which act as 'nurse' crops to the **beech** and are being gradually removed as they mature. **Yew** is plentiful on the steep chalk slopes and the native **box** tree survives in the older woods.

BERKSHIRE

---

21 Cliveden

LOCATION **Two miles (3 km) north of Taplow, on the B476, off the A40;** *Landranger Sheet 175, SU913856;* OPEN **(grounds only) Mar to end-Dec: every day 11-6 or sunset if earlier;** ADMISSION **£2, children £1; Except Mon, Tues and Wed (not bank holiday Mon), when it is £1.50, children £0.75.**

Cliveden is one of the National Trust's largest gardens and the most historically varied. It contains many fine specimen trees, including some 300-year-old **English Oaks** and, along the Cliveden Reach of the River Thames, a famous hanging wood. This was recently decimated not only by elm disease, but also by the drought of 1976; however, an extensive restoration scheme has been carried out.

Highlights

The main phase of landscaping Cliveden began in 1720 with the advice of Charles Bridgeman and much survives from this period. **Limes** were used extensively for avenue planting, and some of these now stand above the general woodland canopy when seen from the terrace, having reached 100 ft (30 m). South of the Long Garden is a unique and beautiful feature – Ilex Grove.

Many of the trees in this plantation of Holm Oak date from the mid-18th C. The Yew Walk, which also dates from the 18th C, is south-west of the house and contains trees of enormous girth.

Yet another giant tree is Cannings **Oak.** Tradition has it that the great statesman, who was a frequent visitor to Cliveden in the early-18th C, often sat beneath it to enjoy the superb view across the River Thames.

Common Beech has dominated the woodlands for 150 years – which reminds one that the estate lies on the edge of the Chiltern Hills. Many mature specimens stand together with **chestnut, sycamore, lime, cherry** and **whitebeam.** Along the river, moisture-loving species such as **Common Alder** are found.

WALES

WEST GLAMORGAN

22 Bishopston Valley

LOCATION The valley runs from Kittle to Pwll-du Bay, 6 miles (10 km) south-west of Swansea; access via the A4067 and the B4436; Landranger Sheet 159, SS575894; OPEN at all times; ADMISSION free.

This is a narrow, steep-sided limestone valley with hanging woods, designated a Site of Special Scientific Interest (SSSI): you will find relatively undisturbed ancient woodlands, marvellous to wander through.

Highlights

At the southern end of the valley, by the coast, are Pwll-du and Lockway Woods, excellently developed ancient coppice woodlands, notable for locally abundant **Small-leaved Lime** as well as a few **Wild Service Trees.** (Both these species are believed to indicate ancient woodland.)

The remainder of the valley is also well wooded and has a fine diversity of habitat. **Ash, hazel, sycamore** and **oak** are present with scattered **Wych Elm.**

DYFED

23 Stackpole

LOCATION Four miles (6.5 km) south of Pembroke; Landranger Sheet 158, SR977963; OPEN at all times; ADMISSION free.

Within the 2,000 acres of this coastal property are both broad-leaved and coniferous woodlands and plantations. Some, such as Shippingback Wood, are sufficiently prominent to be indicated on mariner charts as landmarks. Others are further inland, but one of the main attributes of the area is the diversity of habitats on the woodland edges: they include coastal and fresh water, pasture and cliff. Most of the broad-leaved woodlands were planted in the late-18th C and early-19th C. Of particular interest are areas around the fresh water ponds, and the woodlands around Bolsherton Lakes, especially Lodge Park Wood, which is directly in front of the old Stackpole Court. The Pembrokeshire Coastal Path passes through some of these interesting woodlands.

Highlights

The coastal woodlands around the fresh water ponds in the Stackpole National Nature Reserve make a major contribution to wildlife conservation here. They also offer protection to neighbouring farmland from the salt-laden winds. The deciduous woodlands here, and elsewhere at Stackpole, are mainly **sycamore**- or **ash**-dominated, or a combination of both species. Around Bosherton Lakes are mixed deciduous woodlands; Lodge Park Wood mainly comprises mature **beech** and Holm Oak. **European Larch, hornbeam, willow, English Elm** and an old **yew** are also found.

The young plantations include **poplar** at the Downs and north-east of Stackpole Court; conifers are numerous – those at Castle Dock and Cheriton consisting chiefly of **Grand Fir** and Common Silver Fir with **Monterey Pine** on the upper slopes.

although the southern part of the latter has **oaks** underplanted with conifer. Mature standard **oaks** are found in Ogofau woodland to the west of the Gold Mine, and to the north-east there is a young plantation of Red Oak. To the south is Ogofau carr, which is an **alder**-dominated woodland with some **willow**. Other valley bottoms where **alder** dominates are Llandre Carr and Allt Bwlch y Gilwen.

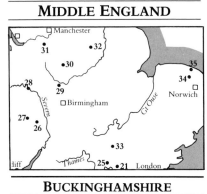

MIDDLE ENGLAND

BUCKINGHAMSHIRE

24 Dolaucothi

LOCATION At Pumsaint, on the A482 road from Lampeter to Llanwrda (A482/A40 junction); *Landranger Sheet 146, SN6640;* OPEN at all times; ADMISSION free.

Dolaucothi Estate is dominated by coppice oakwood, partly underplanted with recent **beech** and conifer plantations. Mature **oak** woodlands surround the Ogofau Gold Mines, originally worked by the Romans.

Highlights

Extensive woodlands run along the valley sides and bottoms of the Afon Cothi and its tributaries. On the valley sides are the **oak** woods, partly underplanted with **beech** and **Western Hemlock.** A typical coppiced western **Sessile Oak** wood is Allt Dinbeth. It is on a steep slope, commanding fine views, and is approached by a marked footpath. Other coppice **oak** woods are Allt Cwm Gerwyn and Allt yr Hebog,

25 Bradenham Woods

LOCATION Immediately north of Bradenham village on both sides of the A4010, 4 miles (6.5 km) northwest of High Wycombe; *Landranger Sheet 165, SU825970;* OPEN at all times; ADMISSION free.

The 380 acres of woods at Bradenham are an excellent example of traditional Chiltern **beech** woods, which used to provide timber for the furniture trade in High Wycombe. It has shallow, chalky soil.

Chiltern beech woods make excellent walking: the light, airy atmosphere under the trees is particularly congenial.

Highlights

These woods are gradually being rejuvenated by a system of small group fellings followed, wherever possible, by natural **beech** regeneration, or by planting **beech** with 'nurse' crops of **European Larch. Wild Cherry** also grows well.

HEREFORD & WORCESTER

26 Brockhampton

LOCATION **Principally on the north side of the road to Worcester (the A44), 2 miles (3 km) east of Bromyard;** *Landranger Sheet 149, SO682546;* OPEN **at all times;** ADMISSION **free.**

Brockhampton has an extensive system of semi-natural woodland broken up mainly with small stream valleys, or dingles. These dingles, often with steep sides, dissect the property and drain eastwards into a tributary of the River Teme. Many of the woodlands along the dingles and on the steeper slopes elsewhere are ancient woodland sites, relatively unmodified by recent planting.

Highlights
In the dingles such as those at Woodcock Hill, Paradise Wood and Limepits Wood **oak, ash** and **hazel** dominate, with **Wych Elm, Small-leaved Lime** and **Wild Service** also present – the last two being typical in local ancient woodlands.

Otherwise the woods contain varied but fewer tree species: for example, Hillfield Coppice is an ancient woodland of **oak** and **ash**; Holy Banks has the best strand of **oak**; and Brockhampton dingle is an ancient **ash** and **Wych Elm** woodland with several large **oaks** and **Small-leaved Limes.**

There are also some mixed secondary woodlands at Brockhampton as well as fairly extensive small plantations of young conifers (**Norway Spruce** and **larch**) scattered around the property, particularly to the east of Brockhampton House.

27 Croft Castle

LOCATION **Five miles (8 km) north-west of Leominster, off the A49;** *Landranger Sheet 137, SO455655;* OPEN **Apr and Oct: Sat, Sun and Easter Mon 2-5. May to end-Sept: Wed to Sun and bank holiday Mon 2-6;** ADMISSION **£1.50, children £0.75.**

This 500-year-old castle has extensive grounds with several interesting features; of particular note are perhaps the very ancient trees growing singly, and in avenues.

Highlights
The first vista to strike the visitor is the irregular avenue of old **oaks** along the approach drive. Even more remarkable, on the south-western boundary, lining an earlier approach, is one of Croft's most famous features – the Chestnut Avenue. This consists of a single line of enormous **Sweet Chestnuts**, weather-beaten and grotesquely contorted, thought to be about 350 years old. For half its length it is flanked by rows of younger, but still massive, trees, and new planting at the eastern end is designed to perpetuate this truly unique collection.

To the west of the house is a very ancient tree, still known as 'Sir Richard's **Oak**'.

Lines of equally ancient specimens can be seen striding across the open farmland to the north of the park, and their arrangement has suggested that they might represent the battle-plan of the Armada, although it is more generally believed that they were planted to celebrate the Restoration.

An avenue of **limes** has recently been established in the centre of the park, also a new avenue of **beeches** approaching the Gothick curtain-wall, replacing old trees which, for safety's sake, had to be felled.

To the north-east of the Castle, reached by footpaths across gently rising farmland, lies the steep-sided Fishpool Valley. The woods surrounding the valley are mainly broad-leaved, with **ash** predominating on the deep alluvial soil near the stream. There are also some fine mature specimens of **Douglas Fir,** which grows exceptionally well on this sheltered site.

SHROPSHIRE

28 Attingham Park

LOCATION **On the north side of the road to Telford (A5), 4 miles (6.5 km) south-east of Shrewsbury;** *Landranger Sheet 126, SJ542093;* OPEN **(deer park and grounds only) all year round: daily during daylight hours;** *Closed* **24 Dec;** ADMISSION **(deer park and grounds only) £0.50, children £0.25.**

The landscaping of Attingham Park began in 1770, when Noel Hill (later first Lord Berwick) commissioned Thomas Leggett to improve the grounds. Leggett created a parkland setting in the style of 'Capability' Brown, with clumps of trees in the open landscape and solid banks of woodland around the boundaries. Noel Hill later built a vast neo-classical mansion surrounding the original building, and it was for this new house that his son, the second Lord Berwick, employed Humphry Repton to devise a further landscaping scheme in 1797. His proposals, contained in a 'Red Book' still at Attingham, were carried out over the following 20 years, and since then few alterations have been made to the landscape. Both Leggett and Repton preferred to use traditional woodland species in the parkland. There are several circular walks, known as the Mile Walk and the Deer Park Walk, which give access to the woods and to the River Tern.

Highlights
There are numerous magnificent specimens of **oak** and **beech** amid these woodlands, which are chiefly mixed broad-leaf. Along the Mile Walk, a naturalized thicket of **Grey Poplars** is found across the River Tern.

29 Dudmaston

LOCATION **Half a mile (0.8 km) north-west of Quatt, on the west side of the road from Bridgnorth to Kidderminster (A442);** *Landranger Sheet 138, SO746887;* OPEN **Apr to end-Sept: Wed and Sun 2.30-6;** ADMISSION **(garden only) £0.80.**

In the Dingle at Dudmaston there is a remnant of the ancient Forest of Morfe. The estate has been in the same family for 850 years; one 20th-C owner, Geoffrey Wolryche-Whitmore, was a pioneer of forestry techniques and responsible for much new planting. As a result, a surprising variety of trees, both broad-leaved and coniferous, are to be found on the estate. The park was landscaped in the 18th C and an extensive garden leads down to the main lake. Most of the woodland lies to the south and west of the park, and there are walks along the lake and through the Dingle, which borders on to the River Severn.

Highlights
Along the walk in the Dingle are some magnificent old specimens of **beech, lime, oak** and **yew.**

Throughout the gardens are several fine mature **Small-leaved Lime** and **English Oak,** and the lake is enhanced by **willow, birch** and **maple.**

DERBYSHIRE

30 Dovedale

LOCATION **West of the A515, 4 to 7 miles (6.5 to 11 km) north-west of Ashbourne;** *Landranger Sheet 119, SK1453;* OPEN **at all times;** ADMISSION **free.**

Dovedale contains one of the finest carboniferous limestone woodlands in the country. This woodland, known as Dovedale Ashwood, is designated an internationally important woodland site; and indeed, most of Dovedale is also a Site of Special Scientific Interest (SSSI).

Highlights
The best and largest area of rich primary woodland is Dovedale Ashwood, between Jacob's Ladder and Ilam Rock. This is about 50 acres, dominated by **ash** and **Wych Elm,** but with some old trees as well as a good selection of native trees. These include **Large-** and **Small-leaved Lime, Field Maple,** Crab Apple, **Bird Cherry** and **spindle.** The crags feature some fine **yews** and Rock Whitebeam.

Other important areas of similarly rich primary woodland are the Nabs and Iron Tors, parts of which also include some fine old trees.

CHESHIRE

31 Styal

LOCATION **One and a half miles (2.5 km) north of Wilmslow, off the B5166;** *Landranger Sheet 109, ST8383;* OPEN **(Country Park only) throughout the year during daylight hours;** ADMISSION **free.**

Although Styal is well known for Quarry Bank Mill, it is now also famed as a marvellous Country Park, set in refreshing and unspoilt countryside within only 10 miles (16 km) of Manchester city centre. It provides access to stretches of the Bollin Valley and pleasant woodlands, notable for their variety of hardwoods.

Highlights

From the main Country Park car park above Quarry Bank Mill, take the footpath leading down the picturesque valley along the east bank of the River Bollin. These woodlands are mostly of **oak** and **beech,** with **willow** and **alder** in wetter areas. Return from Twinnies Bridge along other well signposted paths through Willow Ground Wood and Southern Woods: a pleasant landscape, with beautiful trees.

NOTTINGHAMSHIRE

32 Clumber Park

LOCATION **Four and a half miles (7 km) south-east of Worksop, one mile (1.5 km) from the A1/A57; Landranger Sheet 120, SK645774;** OPEN **at all times;** ADMISSION **pedestrians free, cars £1.40.**

Extending to just under 4,000 acres, Clumber is one of Britain's most visited Country Parks. The park itself was created in the late-18th C by the Dukes of Newcastle out of heathland on the edge of Sherwood Forest. Both Richard Payne Knight and William Sawry Gilpin played an important role in its design. Clumber is best known for its magnificent double **lime** avenue, the longest in the country. The variety of scenery within the grounds and the sheer size means that a whole day can happily

be spent exploring the many miles of gently undulating roads and tracks – perhaps using bicycles, which are available for hire. Near the chapel and lake is a peaceful Victorian pleasure ground with sweeping lawns under large specimen trees.

Highlights

The park contains extensive woods of **oak** and **beech,** with younger plantations including **pine** and **larch.** The famous **lime** avenue, which stretches for some 2½ miles (4 km) from Apley Head to Carburton Lodge, is 60 ft (18 m) wide and comprises a double row of mainly Common Lime planted either side of the road.

Near the main car park are the pleasure grounds extending along the lake. Here you will find clump of common **yew, Large-** and **Small-leaved Lime, hornbeam** and two **Sweet Chestnuts** with superb boles.

HERTFORDSHIRE

33 Ashridge Estate

LOCATION **Either side of the B5406, 3 miles (5 km) north of the road from Berkhamsted to Aylesbury (A41); Landranger Sheet 165, SP970131;** OPEN **at all times;** ADMISSION **free.**

Ashridge Estate comprises about 4,000 acres running along the ridge from Ivinghoe Beacon to Berkhamsted. The woods are scattered astride

the road (B5406), interspersed with farmland and more open areas dominated by **birch.** There are some fine old specimen trees as well as plantations established between the Second World War and the early 1970s.

Highlights

The most common trees are **beech** and **English Oak,** but **Wild Cherry** and **hornbeam** can be found, together with some magnificent **Sweet Chestnuts** of great age.

There are also many young plantations of **beech** and **oak** planted in a matrix of conifers to act as a nurse crop. Although this method has generally succeeded, there are large areas where grey squirrel damage to the hardwoods has been so great that only conifers now remain. These conifers include **Scots** and **Corsican Pine** and **European Larch.** Dense natural **beech** regeneration occurs in the shallow valley below the ancient pollards of Frithsden Beeches.

NORFOLK

34 Blickling Hall

LOCATION **On the north side of the B1354, 1½ miles (2.5 km) north-west of Aylsham; Landranger Sheet 133, TG188275;** OPEN **(park and woods only) at all times;** ADMISSION **(park and woods only) free.**

In the Park and Estate at Blickling, the trees were planted, in groups and singly, to conceal, rather than to enhance, the main house, which is set in a valley. This unusual layout was designed in the early-18th C by one of the owners, Sir John Hobart, and it still dominates today. Another heavily wooded area is the Mount, which was formed by digging out the lake. From here southwards are avenues of mature trees leading towards the house. There are numerous other walks and bridle paths along which to wander in these picturesque surroundings at Blickling, which comprise nearly 5,000 acres. The house itself is Jacobean, well worth a visit, with some interesting historical associations.

Highlights

The most impressive woodland trees are those in the old woodlands, where pollarded **beech, English** and **Sessile Oak** predominate. Many of these are over 200 years old. **Sweet Chestnut** and **Scots Pine** are also present. In plantations established from the early years of this century, **Norway Spruce** and **European** and **Hybrid Larch** grow alongside **oak, Sweet Chestnut, beech** and **Scots Pine.**

The Mausoleum in the park, built *c.*1793, is surrounded by a fine **yew** hedge.

35 Felbrigg Hall

LOCATION **Two miles (3 km) south-west of Cromer, off the A148;** *Landranger Sheet 133, TG193394;* OPEN **(park and woods only) at all times;** ADMISSION **(park and woods) free.**

Considering the sea is only 2 miles (3 km) away, Felbrigg is an oasis of peace and quiet. It is sheltered by the Great Wood, planted in the late-17th C by William Windham, and containing some magnificent, ancient pollarded **beech.** These trees attract a great variety of fungi, including some unique to East Anglia and the area is designated a Site of Special Scientific Interest (SSSI). A well-signposted woodland walk leads through the Great Wood, which runs from the house along the main road from Cromer to Holt – one, in fact, of many walks available for exploring the trees at Felbrigg.

Highlights

Hidden among younger woods at the back of the house are some fine 300-year-old **Sweet Chestnuts,** with spirally twisted bark. Other trees of interest in the Great Wood include some old specimens of **oak** and **Scots Pine;** also **European** and **Japanese Larch** and **Wild Cherry** planted by the late owner in memory of his mother.

He also planted the 'Victory V', two wide rides flanked by young beech trees to commemorate VE Day. Another young plantation is by the picnic area, where **Small-leaved Lime** will be found. Elsewhere in the park look out for **sycamore, White Poplar, hornbeam** and a few mature specimens of **Field Maple,** including one near St Margaret's church, out in the fields beyond the park.

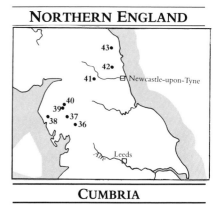

NORTHERN ENGLAND

CUMBRIA

36 Brigsteer Woods

LOCATION **Off the A6, 3½ miles (5.5 km) south of Kendal;** *Landranger Sheet 97, SD498878* OPEN **(garden only) Apr to Oct: Mon, Wed, Fri and Sun 12.30-5.45;** *Closed* **Good Fri;** ADMISSION **(garden only) £0.60.**

Brigsteer Wood occupies 73 acres in the western part of the estate of Sizergh Castle, parts of which date back to the 14th C. About half of the area has been replanted with mixtures of **beech, oak, larch** and **Scots Pine,** and the remainder is preserved as an example of semi-natural coppice woodland, with an abundance of different species. As Brigsteer Wood is situated on a limestone scarp, gradients can be quite steep.

Highlights

The semi-natural woods are the result of a very ancient coppice system, which was finally abandoned in the 1920s. They consist of relict coppice to a height of 15-20 ft (4.5-6 m) and an incomplete canopy of standards, some reaching 40 ft (12 m). The main species of coppice tree is **hazel,** and those of standards, **oak** and **birch. Ash** and **sycamore** are frequently found as both. **Yew** takes advantage of the steeper slopes, whereas **alder** is frequent lower down.

The species of most interest to the enthusiast is Lancastrian Whitebeam – but only one exists in this area. Other species present are Crab, **Small-leaved Lime, hawthorn, holly, rowan** and **Wild Cherry:** a truly varied site.

37 Claife Woods

LOCATION **On the west shore of the northern half of Lake Windermere: cars may be parked along the access road,** ½ **mile (0.8 km) from Ferry Nab;** *Landranger Sheets 96 and 97, SD3898;* OPEN **at all times;** ADMISSION **free.**

Originally **oak-birch** coppiced woodland, as part of the Curwen Estate, Claife Woods were subject to early experimental conifer planting in the late-19th C and to the introduction of exotic species. A pleasant lakeside walk of about 5 miles (8 km) extends from near the Nab as far as Wray Castle, with an alternative of a circular walk of about 6 miles (10 km). This leaves the shore path at Belle Grange to go up the hill and turn left again along the top of the ridge to reach the road at Far Sawrey.

Highlights
In addition to the interesting **Sessile Oak** and **birch** woodland and conifer

plantations, there is also an abundance of **holly,** with **yew** on the crags and **Small-leaved Lime** in the damper areas. **Beech** is present throughout the wood and near Belle Grange the shore path runs through an avenue of mature **Sweet Chestnut.**

38 Nether Wasdale

LOCATION **On both sides of the Wasdale road, 3 m (5 km) northeast of Gosforth, between Bolton Wood (north of the Gosforth to Wasdale road), Santon and Forest bridges (over the River Irt) and Kidbeck Farm (near Nether Wasdale village);** *Landranger Sheet 89, NY115035;* OPEN **at all times;** ADMISSION **free.**

Although much of the area has been planted with **pine, larch** and **Norway Spruce,** Nether Wasdale remains one of the best examples of lowland broad-leaved woodland in the region. Its numerous woods are part of an intricate mosaic of many different types of habitat, and are notable for the range and structure of woodland species to be seen. There is good reason to believe that many of these woods were part of the original forest cover.

Highlights
Approaching the area from the A595 at Gosforth, continue ¼ mile (0.5 km) beyond Peagill. From there, proceed on foot towards Gaterigghow. Some of the richest woodland in the region is to be found here. The **ash-**dominated woods found here along the banks of the River

Irt are some of the richest woodland in the region. Farther on is Mirk Holme – again **ash-**dominated but with **Sessile Oak; alder** coppice is also present. Moving farther east, the **ash** gives way to **Sessile oak;** here Broadgarth Coppice is the site of some fine mature **oaks** and **beeches,** with rich **alder** carr (mostly to the north of the wood).

A similar trend towards oak-domination is seen, moving south. The best example of old oak coppice is Craghouse Wood, close by the hamlet of the same name. This is one of the largest unmodified woods with some splendid old **hollies** and small areas of **willow** and **hazel** carr.

39 Manesty Park

LOCATION **Adjoining the south-west corner of Derwentwater, between Brandelhow and the River Derwent;** *Landranger Sheet 89, NY252192;* OPEN **at all times;** ADMISSION **free.**

Planted on the gentle slopes of Manesty Park are both mature and young trees in a mixed woodland. **Oak** predominates, but scattered through the wood are some magnificent specimens of **European Larch,** which are well worth a visit.

Highlights
In the western part of Manesty Park **Sessile Oak** and **birch** predominate, with frequent mature standard **larch, Scots Pine** and **beech.** Young **beech** and stands of young **larch** and **Scots Pine** occur locally; the **larch** is all

natural regeneration from the outstanding parent trees.

In the more open areas to the east, standard oak predominates; **rowan, birch** and **hawthorn** also thrive there.

40 Great Wood, Derwentwater

LOCATION **Along both sides of the Keswick to Borrowdale road (B5289), 1 mile (1.5 km) south of Keswick;** *Landranger Sheet 89, NY275215;* OPEN **at all times;** ADMISSION **free.**

Here is a mature deciduous woodland split by a central conifer plantation. The mature deciduous woodland, which is a scarce habitat in the north of England, contains some exceptionally fine trees as well as showing characteristics of woodland believed to be associated with the original forest cover of alluvial soils. Indeed, Great Wood is a Site of Special Scientific Interest (SSSI). The most valuable part of the wood is on the lower slopes, west of the conifer area, towards Derwentwater. However, the woodland on the upper slope, by Walla Crags, provides an interesting, and a contrasting woodland type.

Highlights
By the car park are some splendid mature **Wych Elms** as well as **English Oak, beech, ash** and **sycamore.** This flat area by the lake has a variety of different stands. To the north of the car park are some wet areas dominated by two types of **alder** woodland: on the acidic soil, **birch** occurs with **alder:** whereas

elsewhere **Bird Cherry** is found among the **alder** coppice. In the drier areas are seen mature **ash** and **Wych Elm,** often accompanied by old and mature **sycamore** and **beech** and, along the shores of Derwentwater, by **fir** and **pine.** On the steep upper slopes above the conifer plantations grow large coppiced **Sessile Oak** and **ash.**

Of particular interest is one very small area south of the car park, above Cat Gill, which exhibits a gradation of different types of broad-leaved woodland. On the shore line are **ash, Wych Elm** and **hazel;** this then becomes **Sessile Oak** and **hazel** until the 1,000 ft (30 m) contour is reached, when **oak, ash** and **hazel** occur.

NORTHUMBERLAND

41 Allen Banks

LOCATION **South of the road from Hexham to Carlisle (A69), near where the River Allen joins the River Tyne, 3 miles (5 km) west of Haydon Bridge;** *Landranger Sheets 86 and 87, NY799630;* OPEN **at all times;** ADMISSION **free.**

Allen Banks, once part of the Bowes-Lyon Estate at Ridley Hall, comprises 194 acres of mixed woodland, divided by the River Allen. There are approximately 14 miles (22 km) of woodland walks on both sides of the steep valley and these make exploring the area a delight.

Highlights
This is generally mixed woodland with some small plantations of **European Larch** and **Scots Pine** intermixed with **oak, beech** and **sycamore.** There are also some fine specimens of **beech, oak, larch,** and **Douglas Fir** and a number of mature **Sweet Chestnut. Ash, Wild Cherry, birch, rowan** and **yew** are also present. The eastern slopes are covered with mature **Scots Pine, larch** and **oak.** There is also a man-made tarn in this area.

42 Wallington

LOCATION **Either side of the B6342, near Cambo, 12 miles (19 km) west of Morpeth;** *Landranger Sheet 81, NZ030843;* OPEN **(grounds) all year round during daylight hours; (walled garden) every day: Apr to end-Sept: 10-7. Oct: 10-6. Nov to end-Mar: 10-4;** ADMISSION **(walled garden and grounds only) £1.00, children £0.50.**

Wallington boasts much fine woodland in close proximity to the house. Both East and West Woods were laid out with ponds and planted in 1737-8 by Sir Walter Calverly, who was largely responsible for creating the entire park and gardens. More recently successive generations of the Trevelyan family owned Wallington and were involved in enhancing the beauty of the grounds.

Highlights
Wallington contains trees of all ages. On the lawns surrounding the house, for

instance, are young conifer, ancient **hornbeam** (by the ha-ha) as well as **sycamore, Silver Birch,** common **yew** and **Douglas Fir.**

A recently-planted avenue of **Large-leaved Lime** leads towards West Wood, in the north of which are mature **beech** and **oak** with some **holly, ash** and **birch.** Nearer Middle Pond are **ash** and **alder;** elsewhere conifer and mixed young deciduous trees occur.

Over the road, East Wood comprises dense young mixed woodland in the north and south of the Garden Pond, and elsewhere are some fine mature **beech, oak, Douglas Fir** and an immense **larch** (planted 1738). In the field above the walled garden, clumps of native trees have been planted to provide shelter.

survive. There is also a series of artificial lakes above and below the house as well as a medley of intricate paths and well-surfaced drives.

Highlights

The main woodland species are **Scots Pine** and **beech,** but in the sheltered valley below the house are some magnificent specimens of **Douglas Fir** and other western North American conifers, some among the tallest in the country; also **Austrian Pine** and **European Larch.** Nearer the house can be found **Norway Spruce** and **Western Hemlock.**

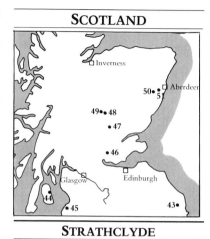

SCOTLAND

STRATHCLYDE

44 Brodick Castle

LOCATION **Two miles (3 km) from Brodick Pier, Isle of Arran. Ferry from Ardrossan (1 hour), bus from harbour;** *Landranger Sheet 69, NR997380;* OPEN **(Country Park and garden only) all year round: daily 9.30-sunset;** ADMISSION **(Country Park and garden only) £0.80, children £0.40.**

Brodick's position on Scotland's west coast means that it has perfect conditions for growing trees: there are no climatic extremes, the garden and Country Park are sheltered, rainfall is heavy and the soil is excellent. Moreover, nowhere else is such a splendid Scottish island garden so accessible. There are some magnificent mature trees, but most of the property has been planted since 1923, by the Duchess of Montrose, her son-in-law, John Boscawen and the National Trust

43 Cragside

LOCATION **One mile (1.5 km) north of Rothbury, on the road to Alnwick (B6341);** *Landranger Sheet 81, NV073022* OPEN **(Country Park) Apr to end-Sept: every day 10.30-6. Oct: every day 10.30-5. Nov to end-Mar: Sat and Sun 10.30-4;** ADMISSION **(Country Park only) £1.00, children £0.50.**

Cragside is set on a steep rocky slope, with informal landscaping right up to the house. Both house and Country Park reflect the genius of the first Lord Armstrong who, between 1864 and 1884, is said to have planted some nine million trees to convert rough moorland into the richly wooded pleasure ground that now exists. Many of these trees still for Scotland. The informal grounds slope away from the castle and formal walled garden down to the sea, and self-guided walks and nature trails are available along many paths.

Highlights

The wide variety of woodland trees includes some particularly fine old specimens of **Sessile Oak** and **Common Beech**. **Elm** is also prevalent and many trees are quite old: Dutch elm disease has, thankfully, not yet reached the island. Look out for some good examples of **Tulip Tree** and **willow**, including **Goat**, or pussy, **Willow** and an immense **birch**. Other broad-leaves of interest, scattered throughout, are **alder, ash, sycamore, rowan,** whitebeam, Sweet Chestnut, Wych Elm, and **magnolia**.

Conifers flourishing here include **Sitka** and **Norway Spruce, Scots** and **Corsican Pine, Japanese** and **European Larch, common yew, Western Hemlock, Douglas Fir** and California Redwood.

45 Culzean

LOCATION **Off the A719, 12 miles (19 km) south-west of Ayr;** *Landranger Sheet 70, NS2310;* OPEN **(Country Park only) all year round; 9-sunset;** ADMISSION **pedestrians free, cars £2.**

Culzean Castle and Country Park stand dramatically on what used to be a bleak and windy stretch of coastline; but in the late-18th C, this unprepossessing site was transformed, possibly by Robinson and Whyte, disciples of 'Capability' Brown. The grounds comprise extensive woods, these are mainly in the east: a mosaic of deciduous stands, typical mixed woodlands and conifer plantations of both mature and young trees. The woodland walks around the Country Park are well worth exploring.

Highlights

Two of the finest indigenous specimens in the grounds are in Happy Valley: they are 150-year-old **Sitka Spruce**. Other particularly impressive trees here include **Scots Pine, Douglas Fir** and **Western Hemlock**.

CENTRAL

46 Dollar Glen

LOCATION **North of Dollar, off the road from Stirling to Kinross (A91);** *Landranger Sheet 58, NS9698;* OPEN **at all times;** ADMISSION **free.**

Dollar Glen is an ancient mixed deciduous woodland through which a dramatic gorge has been carved. It lies on the southern edge of the Ochil Hills, and there are magnificent views from the top of its steep slopes. There is a circular walk through the gorge.

Highlights

Oak predominates on the slopes, but **ash, hazel** and old **sycamore** are also found. Some of the **ash** near the foot of the Glen are among the tallest in Britain.

TAYSIDE

47 The Hermitage

LOCATION **On the A92 to Pitlochry 2 miles (3 km) west of Dunkeld;** *Landranger Sheet 53, NO0041;* OPEN **at all times;** ADMISSION **(honesty box) £0.10, children free.**

A folly, Ossian's Hall, built in 1758, overlooks the beautiful wooded gorge of the River Braan where there are splendid specimens of many coniferous trees, especially **Douglas Fir**. A sign-posted nature trail passes through these outstanding woodlands and plantations.

Highlights

Around the car park are many of the deciduous trees that can be seen during the rest of the walk and which contrast so well with the background conifers. Such broad-leaves as **beech, sycamore, ash, elm, Wild Cherry, oak** and **birch** will be found in this vicinity. From near the folly can be seen one of the tallest trees in Britain, a magnificent 200 ft (61 m) **Douglas Fir.** which is growing on the northern bank of the River Braan.

Further into the wood are **Douglas Fir** and Common Silver Fir, well over a century old and among the finest examples in Britain. One of the **Douglas Firs** across the river just before the pool is one of the tallest in Britain.

After the charming 18th-C bridge and the Hermitage Folly, or Ossian's Hall, the path leads through a much denser wood of **Norway Spruce**. This in turn gives way to **Scots Pine**, with **birch, rowan** and **oak** present.

At Ossian's Cave the path turns inland and here **Norway Spruce** flourish, well spaced out. Where there has been wind damage, natural regeneration of young **beech, rowan, birch, sycamore** and **Douglas Fir** has occurred, but the **Douglas Fir** is now dominant because it grows fastest. **Larch** is found near the railway tunnel, before the return to the car park.

48 Linn of Tummel

LOCATION **On the B8019, 2½ miles (4 km) north-west of Pitlochry; car park at Garry Bridge;** *Landranger Sheet 43, NN9162;* OPEN **at all times;** ADMISSION **free.**

This property is mixed woodland lying at the confluence of the Rivers Garry and Tummel. It is highly characteristic of Perthshire highland woods and contains a fine variety of both broad-leaved and coniferous trees of varying ages. To increase your enjoyment, there is a well sign-posted nature trail to follow through the wood.

Highlights
A bank of well-established **oak** gives way to an interesting assortment of broad-leaves along the strip of woodland between the River Garry and the field. These include **beech, birch, sycamore, ash** and **alder.**

Further on, three distinct types of woodland intersect: **oak,** coniferous and mixed. **Oak** woodland predominates in the bank to the right, while to the left is

a plantation of **Douglas Fir.** The remaining woodland contains a mixed variety of trees, including **European Larch.** Upstream, on the north bank of the River Tummel, there are **Scots Pine** and **birch** with, among others, **oak, hazel, rowan** and **aspen.** The path enters a woodland of **Scots Pine** with scattered conifer plantations of **Douglas Fir, Grand Fir, Norway Spruce** and **Western Hemlock,** and then coppice **hazel** clumps occur. Finally, a **sycamore**-dominated woodland is reached.

49 Pass of Killiecrankie

LOCATION **On the west side of the road from Perth to Inverness (A9), 3 miles (5 km) north of Pitlochry;** *Landranger Sheet 43, NN9162;* OPEN **at all times;** ADMISSION **free.**

At Killiecrankie, the River Garry has cut a narrow gorge through the hills, forcing a pass, which has for many centuries been an important route linking highland and lowland Scotland. Lining the banks is a beautiful ancient woodland of well-mixed deciduous trees. It is a Site of Special Scientific Interest (SSSI). A riverside path runs for a mile from the Soldier's Leap along the east bank, linking up with the Linn of Tummel.

Highlights
Oak and **ash** dominate this dramatic wooded gorge, with **beech, hazel, alder, sycamore** and **birch** also present. **Aspen,** too, is found towards Garry Bridge.

GRAMPIAN

50 Crathes

LOCATION **On the road to Aberdeen (A93), 3 miles (5 km) east of Banchory;** *Landranger Sheets 38 and 45, NO7396;* OPEN **(garden and grounds only) all year: daily 9.30-sunset;** ADMISSION **(garden only) £0.80, children £0.40; (grounds only) £0.50, children £0.25.**

Crathes Castle is set amid a well-wooded estate containing mixed deciduous woodland typical of Royal Deeside, with conifer plantations, a lake and an old sand quarry. The property has been owned by the Burnett family for over 350 years, and there are fine old trees, especially along some of the avenues. To explore fully, use the five well-signposted woodland walks.

Highlights
The original drive to the castle was West Avenue, which comprised lime, **sycamore, oak** and **beech** – some of which are still standing. However, the limes in the avenues alongside the Walled Garden have recently been replanted: the old trees had become dangerous with age. Along the main entrance, East Avenue, are various woodland trees, including **oak, beech, Wych** and **Smooth-leaved Elm, Sweet Chestnut, whitebeam** and **hornbeam** – the last being fairly unusual in this region.

In the quarry grow **Silver Birch, rowan** and **Wild Cherry** and farther west, along Ley Way, are seen **Scots Pine** on the rocky outcrops by the old drive.

The various woodland walks wander among native broad-leaves such as **Common Alder, ash, Downy Birch, Goat,** or pussy, **Willow** and **White Willow. Douglas** and **Grand Fir, Sitka** and **Norway Spruce** and **larch** also thrive throughout the grounds.

51 Drum Castle

LOCATION **Off the road from Aberdeen to Banchory (A93), 3 miles (5 km) west of Peterculter;** *Landranger Sheet 38, NJ7900;* OPEN **(grounds only) all year round: daily 9.30-sunset;** ADMISSION **(grounds only) by donation.**

The grounds at Drum Castle encompass part of the Old Forest of Drum, which is unique in being the only block of mature oak woodland on lower Deeside. It is also a Site of Special Scientific Interest (SSSI). The Old Forest has been a woodland site for many centuries – mature **oak** being recorded there during the 17th C, and it is the oldest extant portion of the Caledonian Forest in the eastern coastal area of Scotland. A woodland walk has been laid out through part of the Old Forest. Drum Castle also has a pleasant parkland dotted with fine old indigenous trees.

Highlights
The Old Forest is dominated by **English Oak** but **Scots Pine, beech, Wild Cherry** and **Wych Elm** are present, too. The roots of many fallen **oak** and

Scots Pine can also be seen. These trees were the sad victims of a gale in 1953 – the Forest stands in fairly shallow soil with an underlying hardpan of crushed granite.

An arboretum near the castle contains a few more woodland tree species: **sycamore, Sweet Chestnut, English Elm,** whitebeam, **Norway Maple, Douglas** and **Grand Fir, Western Hemlock, Monterey Pine** and **Norway Spruce.** Also growing at Drum, scattered in the parkland outside the arboretum, are **Silver** and **Downy Birch, Common Ash, rowan,** lime, holly, **Japanese Larch** and **yew.**

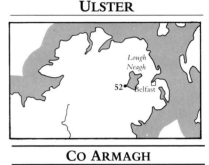

ULSTER

CO ARMAGH

52 The Argory

LOCATION **On the Derrycaw road, 3 miles (5 km) from Coalisland intersection (Junction 14) of the M1;** *Landranger Sheet 00, HS872580;* OPEN **(grounds only) Apr to end-Sept: daily 8.30-7. Oct to end-Mar: daily 8.30-dusk;** ADMISSION **(grounds only) free.**

Some of the finest **oak** and **beech** in Northern Ireland can be observed at the Argory, in which over 200 acres of this 315-acre estate are woodland, including impressive old **oak** woods. The grounds overlook the Blackwater River and contain a number of interesting woodland walks.

Highlights
A peat bog, unworked for 25 years, is of particular interest since it has unevenaged, natural regneration of **oak** and **Scots Pine.** Fine examples of **Sweet Chestnut, Spanish Chestnut, lime, birch** and **elm** can also be seen throughout the estate, also an excellent form of **Scots Pine.**

REPUBLIC OF IRELAND

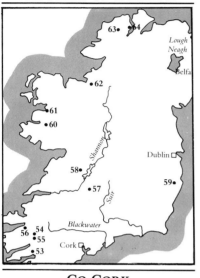

adapted to constant moisture. Area of Scientific Interest (ASI) of international importance. Most natural woods at head of valley.

55 Muckross Wood/ Old Kenmare Road

LOCATION Four-and-a-half miles (7 km) south of Killarney on N71 (T65) to Kenmare. Turn right before entrance to Torc Waterfall.

Killarney **oak** woods; also Strawberry Tree and finest **yew** wood in Ireland. *Sorbus anglica* on lake shore. Area of Scientific Interest (ASI) of international importance.

56 Caragh Lake

LOCATION Five miles (8 km) south-west of Killorglin on 3rd-class road to Caragh Lake. On north-east shore of lake, adjacent to Lake Field.

Native **oak** woodland. Area of Scientific Interest (ASI) of national importance.

CO LIMERICK

57 Glenstal

LOCATION Travel 3 miles (5 km) east of Newport on R503 (T19) to Thurles. Turn right for 2 miles (3 km) on 3rd-class road to Moroe.

Wet woodland with **oak** and **Bird Cherry.** Area of Scientific Interest (ASI) of regional importance.

CO CLARE

58 Cahermurphy

LOCATION Adjacent to Flagmount village on shores of Lough Graney.

Oak wood, with **birch** and **holly.** Area of Scientific Interest (ASI).

CO WICKLOW

59 Avondale Forest Park

LOCATION Two miles (3 km) south of Rathdrum on R752 (T7) to Arklow. On left-hand side of road.

Comprehensive collection of conifers and broad-leaves including species introduced by Augustine Henry; also semi-natural **oak** woods.

CO GALWAY

60 Lough Inagh

LOCATION Five miles (8 km) north of Recess on road to Kylemore.

CO CORK

53 Glengarriff

LOCATION Adjacent to Glengarriff on N71 (T65) to Kenmare.

Oak, birch, rowan, Strawberry Tree. Area of Scientific Interest (ASI) of international importance.

CO KERRY

54 Derrycunnihy/Ladies View

LOCATION Eleven miles (17.5 km) south of Killarney on N71 (T65) to Kenmare.

Oak-holly wood in its classical form

Old semi-natural **oak** woodland. Area of Scientific Interest (ASI) of national importance.

CO MAYO

61 Old Head

LOCATION **Two miles (3 km) northeast of Louisburg close to the R335.**

Rare example of coastal Atlantic **oak**wood with rich lichen. Area of Scientific Interest (ASI).

CO SLIGO

62 Union Wood

LOCATION **Five miles (8 km) south of Sligo on the R284 (L3).**

Typical western **oak**wood with **holly** and **rowan.** Most important **oak** wood in county. (ASI) of national importance.

CO DONEGAL

63 Mullangore Wood

LOCATION **On the slopes of Kinneveagh on the south-eastern shores of Lough Beagh, within Glenveagh National Park, Letterkenny.**

This natural woodland is believed to be a relic of the woods that once covered Donegal. **Sessile Oak** and **Silver Birch** predominate, with **holly, rowan** and **yew** also present.

64 Rathmullan Wood/ Hollymount

LOCATION **One mile (1.5 km) southwest of Rathmullen on R247 (L77) to Rathmelton, on west shore of Lough Swilly.**

Mature deciduous woodland-**oak** and **beech** and **birch** scrub. Area of Scientific Interest (ASI) of local importance.

Britain's changing landscape

The vegetation cover provided by trees, shrubs and other plants in what is now the British Isles has varied dramatically over the millions of years of geological time.

Some 310 to 290 million years ago, the climate was equatorial, and luxuriant rain forest covered much of the land. The remains of this forest, with its gigantic club-mosses up to 100 ft (30 m) tall and great tree ferns and horsetail plants, eventually formed the coal seams that are mined today.

Scorching deserts

By about 290 million years ago, Sahara-like conditions prevailed. Most vegetation had disappeared and there were vast areas of sand-dunes, which today form the sandstones of areas such as south-east Devon.

Sub-tropical forest flourished some 140 to 120 million years ago. Conifers, ferns and horsetails, along with palm-like cycads, were the main plants, for true flowering plants did not appear until about 95 million years ago.

A land bridge joined Britain to the rest of Europe for much of geological time, and across this bridge, tree and plant species spread. By about 35 million years ago, Britain's rich and varied cover included magnolias, giant redwoods and palms. All this was to change during the coming Ice Age.

The northern ice sheets began to edge southwards about 2 million years ago. They were to advance and retreat several times, and as they advanced, tree and plant species moved southwards, returning northwards as the ice sheets retreated. At the time of their maximum extent, about 400,000 years ago, the ice sheets covered virtually all of Britain north of the Thames and the Severn estuary, and only a few mosses managed to survive in the tundra to the south of this cold frontier line.

Retreat of the ice

The ice began its last withdrawal about 15,000 years ago, and the temperate climate of today developed. Trees and plant species re-invaded northern Europe and spread into Britain, and our native trees, shrubs and plants date from this time. **Willow,** dwarf **birches** and **juniper** were the vanguard of the advancing forest. **Birches** and **pines** followed. Later, as the climate began to resemble that of today, broad-leaved forests including **oak, Wych Elm, hazel** and **alder** became established.

However, the sea level was rising as the ice melted, and about 7,500 years ago Britain was severed from the Continent as the sea broke through to make the Strait of Dover. Many European tree species, including the **Norway Spruce** (the 'Christmas tree'), **European Larch** and European silver fir, did not have time to reach Britain before the land bridge disappeared. As a result, our range of native trees is very limited compared with what it was in the past, totalling only 35 tree species and a few shrubs.

A land of vast forests

Successive waves of migrant peoples from the Continent crossed to Britain. The earliest were Stone Age hunters and gatherers who, even with their primitive stone tools, made the first inroads on Britain's forests. About 3,500 BC, people with a more settled way of life based on farming arrived. Their methods of cultivation rapidly intensified the clearance of woodland, and this clearance was to continue at an increasing rate for the next 4,000 years.

The early farmers found about two-thirds of Britain covered by trees. There was dense forest, largely of **oak** and **alder,** on the fertile lowlands and wet valley bottoms, while more open woodland of **Sessile Oak, lime, birch** and **hazel** covered the south and east. **Scots Pine, Sessile Oak** and **juniper** clothed the uplands of the north and west.

Sharp-edged tools of flint enabled the farmers of the 'New Stone Age' to fell trees for fuel, to provide building material for their primitive houses, and to make clearings in which to graze their livestock and grow their crops, including barley and oats. These clearings were most easily made and maintained in the open woodlands on the dry chalk and limestone soils of the south-east. It is in these regions that the tree cover has been removed for the longest time and where soils are therefore thin and poor.

Many of the raw materials available to prehistoric man came from trees and shrubs, and he very early learned how to produce staple items from wood. For instance, the coppicing of **hazel** and other species provided long straight rods for the fences needed to protect and contain livestock.

Axes of bronze, sharper and more durable than those of flint, were common in Britain by about 1,000 BC and must have contributed considerably

119

to the destruction of woodland. More efficient tools of iron helped the Celts, who began arriving in Britain about 500 BC, to carve out even more farmland from the virgin forests.

Destruction of woodland probably increased during the Roman occupation. The Romans removed broad swathes of trees and shrubs alongside their roads to prevent them being used as cover by enemies.

Land-hungry Saxon farmers

However, it was the Saxons who cleared Britain's ancient forests most thoroughly, as they laid down a pattern of farming communities that survived into recent times. So successful were they that when the Domesday Book was compiled for William the Conqueror in 1086, on the basis of a nation-wide survey of resources, it disclosed that only 20 per cent of England was still covered by forests. This was the first written estimate of the extent of Britain's tree cover.

The Normans, with their love of the chase, found it necessary to designate certain areas as 'Royal Forests'. Several of these royal hunting preserves, including the New Forest and Forest of Dean, survive today as areas that were probably always wooded.

Dwindling forest resources

During the following centuries, many factors conspired to deplete Britain's forests even more, and to prevent land cleared of trees from reverting to woodland. By Tudor times exports of wool were vital to the economy of the energetic and ambitious nation that England had become. Large parts of the country, particularly the Cotswolds, were used for grazing sheep, and young tree seedlings and saplings stood little chance against the voracious animals. Scotland, too, was a mainly pastoral nation, and by 1500 most of the great Caledonian **pine** forest had been destroyed.

South-east Britain also suffered. Extensive ship-building in the reigns of Henry VIII and Elizabeth I led to the destruction of much of the **oak** forest of the Kent and Sussex Weald. The production of charcoal for the area's flourishing iron industries and the building of timbered Wealden houses also played their part.

Even before its heyday in Tudor and Elizabethan times, the wool trade led to the enclosure of great tracts of Saxon open fields to provide pastures. At first, wattle fences checked the flocks, but the planting of hedgerows followed as a means of demarcating boundaries. These were often of **hawthorn,** and furnished an ideal environment in which other trees could grow. In this way Britain's vast mileage of hedgerows with trees – such a dominant feature of many landscapes today – came into being.

However, there was little incentive for people to try to re-establish Britain's forests as they had existed in earlier centuries. Even in the 18th and 19th centuries, when the Industrial Revolution greatly increased the demand for timber, the country was wealthy enough to buy from abroad.

The successful industrial families of the time often spent much of their wealth in the countryside, establishing landed estates, but they were not interested in replacing woodland, for which there was scant need. Instead, they employed architects such as Capability Brown to supervise extensive ornamental tree planting, which added to the variety of trees in the landscape.

Hope for the future

It was not until the First World War that home-grown timber was needed again in any quantity. The German blockade prevented imports; large-scale tree felling on private estates ensued, and by 1918 only some 4 per cent of Britain was still covered with woodland.

This state of affairs led to the setting up in 1919 of the Forestry Commission to undertake a national forestry programme and to encourage private owners in commercial timber production. Today, despite extensive tree-felling in the Second World War, about 9 per cent of the island carries productive woodland and forest.

Trees and man

If a farmer from pre-Roman times were to return to Britain today, he would be amazed at the variety of trees and shrubs growing in the countryside. He would recognise only about one in five of the species, for the rest have been introduced since his day from other parts of the world.

It was the Romans who began the diversification of Britain's treescape. The ever-practical conquerors brought in the **walnut, Sweet Chestnut** and stone pine, probably for the sake of their edible seeds. Other trees which they may have introduced include the **sycamore** and Holm Oak.

In the Middle Ages, as contact between Britain and the Continent increased, more and more trees were shipped to a 'second home' in Britain. Monks were constantly in touch with their European counterparts and probably introduced fruit and timber trees for their economic value, though no record of particular species exists.

About 100 years before the birth of Elizabeth I the **Norway Spruce** – the now familiar Christmas tree – was introduced. Other introductions took place in the Elizabethan age, including the medlar from southern Europe and the Black Mulberry from Asia, both of which were wanted for their fruit. The Common Silver Fir arrived in 1603, and in 1616 the **Horse Chestnut** was brought from Greece or Albania. It was followed by the **European Larch**, which is thought to have been brought back from Russia by John Tradescant around 1618 – 11 years before he became gardener to Charles I. Tradescant also persuaded ships' captains bound for North America to bring back tree seeds.

His son, John Tradescant junior, later sailed across the Atlantic and between them they introduced many American trees, including the Locust Tree in about 1636, Swamp Cypress around 1640, and the Tulip Tree some ten years later.

Conifers from North America

Throughout the 17th and 18th centuries, gardeners and botanists were commissioned by wealthy patrons to collect the seeds of ornamental trees and shrubs. One such patron was Peter Collinson, a successful London draper, who planted many North American trees in his garden near Hendon, North London. The land now forms part of the grounds of Mill Hill School, and some of the trees – including a Swamp Cypress, a Cedar of Lebanon, an oriental plane and a magnificent Holm Oak – are still standing. Also from North America came conifers such as the **Douglas Fir** and the **Sitka Spruce.**

Similar collections were made by the Botanic Gardens of Oxford and Edinburgh, and by the Oregon Association, formed by Scotsmen in the mid-19th century to exploit the natural products of North America. The Horticultural Society of London, founded in 1804, sent David Douglas to the west coast conifer forests of North America. In the late 1820s he was the first person to collect the seeds of the **Douglas Fir,** which was named after him, the Noble and **Grand Firs,** and numerous other trees. More than 20 years later the Oregon Association sent John Jeffrey – who, like Douglas, was a native of Perthshire – to California, from where he sent back several species, including Jeffrey's pine and **Western Hemlock.**

Although China and Japan were not open to European travellers until the end of the 19th century, the Tree of Heaven was discovered in China by a French monk named Pierre d'Incarville, who had been allowed into the country as a missionary, and was introduced to Britain in 1751. Seven years later it was followed by the Maidenhair Tree, or ginkgo, which came from China via Japan. The **Japanese Larch** arrived in 1861, when it joined other oriental trees such as the Chinese juniper, the Chinese fir and the graceful deodar cedar, the last of which arrived from Kashmir in 1829.

Ornamentals from the Orient

Another collector who introduced ornamental trees long cultivated in the Far East was the Cornishman, William Lobb, who worked for the enterprising nursery firm of James Veitch. Lobb was rivalled by Robert Fortune of the Horticultural Society, and between them they were responsible for the introduction of many trees, including the Japanese Red Cedar in 1842. Delavay's Silver Fir was introduced from China by Father Jean Marie Delavay at the beginning of the 20th century.

One of the most valuable acquisitions was made in 1904 by Henry 'Chinese' Wilson, who brought the Handkerchief or Dove Tree to England. China also provided Britain's most recent introduction, the Dawn Redwood (1946). It was previously known as a fossil and was not found living in China until 1941. Today its bronze autumn foliage enriches many gardens and tree collections.

Trees for pleasure and profit

Many of the treescapes planned by the great landscape gardeners of the 18th century can still be seen today; and it was also in the 18th century that private landowners first started the extensive planting of conifers typical of modern commercial timber forests.

The 'natural look', in which gardens were an extension of the countryside, was pioneered early in the 18th century by the Yorkshireman, William Kent – the acknowledged father of English gardening. He was succeeded by his pupil Lancelot 'Capability' Brown, a Northumbrian who gained his nickname from his habit of riding round a site that he was about to redesign and listing its 'capabilities' for improvement. He rejected formal features such as straight avenues in favour of clumps of trees and winding lakes.

Brown remodelled or laid out the grounds of the Palladian villa of Nuneham, near Oxford, as well as those at Kew and Blenheim Palace, Oxfordshire, the home of the Duke of Marlborough – all of which are open to the public today.

On Capability Brown's death in 1783 his mantle was donned by Humphry Repton, a failed general merchant and unsuccessful investor. He developed his own technique, in which he sketched the faults of an estate and then provided an overlay drawing which showed his potential clients the 'before and after' effect. His first major creation was at Cobham Hall, Kent, around 1790. Today the 50 acres of grounds are open to the public, and the specimen trees growing there include some giant **cedars.** Repton added more detail to the

long vistas of his predecessors, and he was employed by many of the leading noblemen of his day.

Tree planting in the 18th century was not all for ornament. Some had a practical purpose, and trees originally introduced from abroad for their botanical interest were eventually used for their timber as well. Early in the 18th century Lord Weymouth extensively planted at Longleat in Wiltshire the eastern American white pine that was to be named after him in Britain. At about the same time the 3rd Duke of Atholl – the owner of large Perthshire estates – began the widespread planting of **European Larch,** earning himself the nickname of 'the planting duke'. He and his successors planted some 27 million trees. The most successful introductions of all were the many conifers brought over from the west coast of North America, which are now Britain's most highly valued timber trees.

For a long time private landowners were alone in exploiting the potential of such introduced trees, and they did it only to a limited extent. However, following the acute timber shortage of the First World War, the Forestry Commission was set up in 1919 to establish supplies of home-grown timber. It achieved this by planting on marginal uplands, and by helping private owners to regenerate their woods and to establish new ones.

Timber and recreation

In the last 60 years British foresters have pioneered nursery practices, from seed-sowing to soil management, and have

introduced special afforestation techniques to establish the seedlings on what would once have been regarded as unsuitable ground. In such activities as nursery work, the ploughing of forest land and deep draining, Britain is ahead of many countries with longer forestry traditions. Home-grown forest products are coming onto the market in increasing sizes and quantities, and are beginning to create paper-pulping, board-making and new saw-milling industries in this country.

The introduction of trees has benefited Britain in many ways, not least of which is that plantations provide the public with places for recreation. Walking, horse-riding, bird-watching and path-finding are all the more enjoyable in a forest setting – provided that visitors respect the surroundings and appreciate that the area's main purpose is the production of timber.

The age of trees

The oldest living things in the world are trees: short, twisted bristle-cone pines in the White Mountains of California, North America, which have been standing for nearly 5,000 years. They were already more than 1,000 years old when the Ancient Greek civilisation first stirred into life about 1200 BC. Nearly as long-lived are the massive Wellingtonias of California, which are known to have survived for 3,400 years.

Britain's longest-lived tree is the **yew**, which can reach an age of more 1,000 years, although few standing today are as old as this. Many **yew** trees have several younger stems growing round a long-dead central stem, leaving a hollow centre. The Fortingall Yew near Aberfeldy in Tayside, Scotland, has just such a hollow shell. Reputedly Britain's oldest tree, it is believed to be at least 1,500 years old, and may have been a sapling in Roman times.

Trees of 100-200 years old are not uncommon, and there are still some healthy **oaks** and **Sweet Chestnuts** in British parks and gardens that have been standing for four or five centuries.

How rings are formed

When a tree growing in a temperate climate such as that of Britain is cut down, a series of rings can be seen on the stump of the tree and on the end of the severed trunk. Each ring marks one year's growth.

Trees grow only in the warmer part of the year – generally from March to October – and the growth of the woody parts in spring differs from growth in summer. In spring, thin walled cells with large central spaces are formed to conduct water and minerals (sap) from the roots to the rapidly growing parts of the tree. In summer, cells with thicker walls are formed to give strength to the new growth.

The thin-walled spring wood is lighter in colour than the thick-walled summer wood, and although the two merge during a year's growth, the dark summer wood formed at the end of the growing season shows up distinctly against the light spring wood of the following season, so forming a ring.

Telling the age of a living tree

Annual rings are not necessarily all evenly spaced. They reveal not only the tree's age but also its history – showing, for example, a year of drought when growth was limited and the ring narrow.

It is possible to count the annual growth rings in a living tree. This is done with an instrument called an increment borer, which is driven into the trunk straight towards the centre. It cuts out a core of wood about as thick as a pencil, and when this is pulled out the number of rings can be counted.

Another way of finding the age of a larger tree is by measuring the girth of its trunk at a height of about 5 ft (1.5 m) above the ground. Even though an old tree will cease to grow in height, it must continue to form annual rings, so its girth expands throughout its life.

A tree with a full crown expands by about 1 in (2.5 cm) in girth each year, if growing in uncrowded conditions. Trees growing in a wood in competition with others take about two years to expand by the same amount, and those partially confined in, say, an avenue take about one and a half years.

Although young trees usually grow faster, and old trees slower, than 1 in. (2.5 cm) a year, this is the average expansion. So a tree with a girth of about 8 ft (2.5 m) growing in the open is probably about 100 years old.

Coniferous trees

The age of a coniferous tree can also be assessed by its branch pattern, a method that is accurate while it is still fairly young. The branches occur in whorls – several growing out almost horizontally round the stem at the same height. Such whorls can be seen on all conifers up to 40 or 50 years of age, except Cypresses.

The whorls are formed from side buds grouped round the base of the leading bud, and each spring all the buds develop into branches. Each whorl of branches is therefore separated by a length of stem developed from the leading bud, and the whorl and the stem above it are one year's growth.

A tree's age can be found by counting the whorls, but it is always safest to allow a few extra years for lower branches that may have been lost in early life. Branches that have been cut off usually leave a scar that can be seen for many years. A whorl of scars indicates the beginning of a year's growth.

On occasions, however, a tree will develop two whorls in one year. This may ocur in a season with a long summer and mild autumn, when buds that have developed during summer for the following season's growth are stimulated by the good weather to open in late August.

Glossary

A

Abscission layer Cork layer forming at base of leaf-stalk of DECIDUOUS tree in autumn, causing leaf to fall.

Alternate Term used of leaves or buds of broad-leaved trees that arise first on one side of a twig, then on the other.

Annual ring Ring of wood laid down in stem and branches of tree or shrub during one growing season.

Arboretum A botanical tree garden.

Aril Fleshy cup formed from fused CONE SCALES.

B

Bark Protective layer on the outside of stems and branches, consisting of living cork cells on the inside and dead cells on the outside.

Bract scale Thin, papery, seed-bearing structure rising from CONE AXIS.

Branchlet Small branch, between branch and twig in size.

Bud scale Scale that covers and protects a developing leaf.

C

Cambium Layer of living cells just under bark and at growing tips of shoots and roots, from which new growth develops.

Carr Copse on boggy ground or fenland.

Catkin Male or female flowers hanging in chains; they lack coloured petals because they are wind-pollinated.

Clone Identical plant arising from a single parent by VEGETATIVE PROPAGATION.

Compound Term describing leaf that consists of several LEAFLETS.

Cone axis Central core of cone.

Cone scale Woody structure rising from CONE AXIS, enclosing developing seeds.

Coniferous Term describing tree that bears cones.

Coppicing Cutting of woody stem at ground level to encourage growth of several stems from one root system.

Cotyledon SIMPLE leaf formed in the seed; the first to emerge on GERMINATION. Also called seed leaf.

Cross-fertilisation FERTILISATION of the OVULE of one individual plant by the pollen from another.

Crown Branches and upper part of trunk of tree.

Cultivar Variation of a SPECIES arising in cultivation, and propagated for some unusual characteristic such as leaf colour or shape.

Cuticle Waxy surface of a leaf, reducing water loss and protecting against damage.

D

Deciduous Term describing tree or shrub that retains its leaves for one growing season only.

E

Entire Term describing leaf without lobes, teeth or other indentations in margin.

Evergreen Tree or shrub that retains its leaves all year.

F

Family Large group of similar plants, made up of several genera (see GENUS).

Fastigiate A tree with nearly vertical branches.

Fertilisation Union of a male pollen grain with a female OVULE to form the embryo of a new individual.

G

Genus Group of closely related plants distinct enough not to interbreed. Usually consists of several SPECIES. Plural: genera.

Germination Development of seedling from fertilised seed.

Glaucous Term describing waxy film on the surface of a leaf or stem, giving it a bluish appearance and serving to reduce water loss.

Grafting Artificial union of the aerial parts of one plant with the vigorous ROOTSTOCK of another.

H/I

Hanging wood Woodland growing up steep slope.

Hardy Tolerant of adverse conditions of climate and soil.

Heartwood Dead wood consisting of several ANNUAL RINGS at centre of tree trunk or branch, no longer water-conducting tissue but providing structural support.

Hybrid Offspring of CROSS-FERTILISATION.

Indigenous Native.

L

Lateral roots Shallow roots running out sideways from stem.

Layering Term describing the development of a new individual plant from a branch or stem that has rooted into the ground.

Leading shoot Main shoot that develops from the terminal bud at the top of a tree each year.

Leaflet Leaf-shaped subdivision of a COMPOUND leaf.

Lenticel Small PORE in bark.

Lobe Rounded indentation on leaf margin.

N

Native A species which is thought to have reached Britain since the Ice Age without the aid of man.

Nutlet Small nut, usually one of several in the same fruit.

O

Opposite Term used of buds or leaves of broad-leaved trees that are arranged in pairs on the twig.

Ovule Unfertilised, rudimentary seed of a flowering plant.

P

Perfect Term describing a flower with both male and female parts.

Persistent Term describing part of a plant that does not fall, wither or disappear, as is usual with the some parts of other plants.

Petals Parts of PERFECT and female flower that surround the reproductive organs. They are often coloured to attract insects.

Photosynthesis Chemical process carried out by green plants in presence of light, which combines carbon dioxide from the atmosphere with hydrogen from water in the soil to form sugars as food for the growing plant.

Pinetum ARBORETUM planted with coniferous trees.

Pinnate Term used of leaf completely subdivided into several LEAFLETS ranged along either side of midrib.

Pollarding Lopping of the topmost branches of a tree to encourage shoots to arise all at the same level.

Pollen Fine yellow grain from male flowers or male parts of PERFECT flowers that fertilises the female OVULE.

Pore Area of thin-walled cells in the surface of a leaf or in bark that permits exchange of oxygen and carbon dioxide between the tree and the atmosphere.

Pulvinus Base of a leaf-stalk: the swollen part of a shoot from which a leaf arises.

R

Respiration Exchange of oxygen from the atmosphere with carbon dioxide formed in a plant when energy is released from stored foods: the reverse of PHOTOSYNTHESIS.

Root hairs Fine structures at tips of young roots, through which water and mineral salts are absorbed from soil.

Rootstock Root of common plant on to which a less common plant is joined by GRAFTING.

S

Sapwood Living wood consisting of outer ANNUAL RINGS in tree trunk, through which water from soil is conducted up a tree.

Scale See BRACT, SCALE, BUD SCALE, CONE SCALE.

Scrub Ground covered with brushwood or stunted forest growth.

Seed Small, usually rounded body, sometimes with a wing to aid wind dispersal, that develops from the FERTILISATION of the OVULE, and from which a new plant develops after GERMINATION.

Seed leaf See COTYLEDON.

Sepal Scale, similar to BUD SCALE, but covering and protecting the developing flower.

Short shoot Shoot which extends only a little each year.

Simple Term describing a leaf that is not divided into LEAFLETS.

Species Group of plants similar in all respects and able to interbreed.

Springwood Inner part of ANNUAL RING, formed early in growing season, consisting of thin-walled vessels for conducting water.

Stipule Leaf-like growth on stem at base of leaf-stalk, often in pairs.

Stomata Breathing PORES in leaves, often concentrated on underside; they may give leaves a GLAUCOUS appearance.

Summerwood Outer part of ANNUAL RING, formed during middle and later part of growing season, consisting of thick-walled vessels for conducting water up the stem.

T

Tap root Main downward-growing root of seedling.

Taxa (plural of taxon) General term for any unit of classification, be it form, variety, species, genus, family and so on; mostly used when speaking of several such categories at the same time.

Tooth One of a series of small, regular points on a leaf margin.

V/W

Variety Variation of a SPECIES arising in the wild, usually differing in only one characteristic, such as colour or leaf shape.

Vegetative propagation Reproduction by CUTTINGS, LAYERING and GRAFTING; not involving FERTILISATION.

Whorl Structures such as buds and leaves arising three or more at a time around a stem at the same point.

Index

TREES

SITES

Acknowledgements

The editor and publishers would like to thank the following for their invaluable help in compiling information for this book:

Dr T.W. Wright, adviser on Conservation and Woodlands, The National Trust.

Staff of The National Trust, in particular head gardeners, regional foresters, regional information officers, administrators and land agents who supplied information and answered queries.

Graeme Morison, Michael Blacklock and Judy Aitken of The National Trust for Scotland.

Staff of The National Trust for Scotland, especially principals, ranger-naturalists and resident representatives, who supplied information and answered queries.

Richard Webb, An Taisce (National Trust for Ireland).

Sara Shepley, Centre Manager, Witley Common Information Centre, The National Trust, for her feature on Basic Fieldcraft.

Editorial and design
Researched and written by Joanna Chisholm; assistant editor Rosemary Dawe; designed by Arthur Brown; map on page 96 by Line and Line.

WOODLAND TREES & SHRUBS
is based on the Reader's Digest Field Guide to the Trees and Shrubs of Britain
to which the following made major contributions:

CONSULTANTS AND AUTHORS
Esmond Harris, B.Sc., Dip. For., F.I. For., Director, The Royal Forestry
Society of England, Wales and Northern Ireland
Jeanette Harris, B.Sc.

ARTISTS

Dick Bonson	Charles Raymond
Brian Delf	Derek Rodgers
Shirley Felts	Jim Russell
Ian Garrard	David Salariya
Nick Hall	Ann Savage
Delyth Jones	Bruce Whatley

The publishers would also like to thank The Royal Forestry Society of England, Wales and Northern Ireland for its valuable and expert assistance in the preparation of this book